CURRENT ISSUES BIBLE STUDY SERIES

The Future of the Church

INTERNATIONAL

THOMAS NELSON
Since 1798

NASHVILLE   DALLAS   MEXICO CITY   RIO DE JANEIRO   BEIJING

OTHER BOOKS IN THIS SERIES

Engaging Culture
Islam
Politics
Faith and Work
Faith and Pop Culture
Creation Care
The Bible

Current Issues Bible Study Series: The Future of the Church
Copyright © 2008 *Christianity Today* International

Unless otherwise indicated, Scripture taken from the HOLY BIBLE, NEW CENTURY VERSION®, Copyright © 2005 by Thomas Nelson, Inc. Used by permission. All rights reserved.

All rights reserved. No portion of this book may be reproduced, stored in a retrieval system, or transmitted in any form or by any means—electronic, mechanical, photocopy, recording, scanning, or other—except for brief quotations in critical reviews or articles, without the prior written permission of the publisher.

Editor: Kelli B. Trujillo
Development Editors: Kelli B. Trujillo and Roxanne Wieman
Associate Editor: JoHannah Reardon
Page Designer: Robin Crosslin

ISBN 13: 978-1-4185-3411-0

Printed in the United States of America
09 10 11 12 RRD 5 4 3 2 1

CONTENTS

Contributing Writers 7

Introduction 9

Session 1: The Church in the Twenty-First Century 12
As our world changes, what should—and shouldn't—change about the church?

Session 2: Plant a Church, Make a Convert 28
Is church planting the new (old) wave of evangelism?

Session 3: Tradition: Love it or Lose it? 42
Do the traditions of the past make for a healthy church of the future—or do they breed an empty faith?

Session 4: The Emerging Future Church? 60
Is emerging Christianity the answer to postmodern challenges?

Session 5: Multiracial Congregations 78
Is it possible to overcome our racial barriers and be the unified church God has called us to be?

Session 6: First Responders 96
What is our responsibility in a world filled with disasters, terrorism, and tragedy?

Session 7: Embracing Orthodoxy 110
How will the faith of today's younger generations shape the face of the future church?

Session 8: Loving the Imperfect Church 128
Why should we stick it out with a flawed body of believers?

CONTRIBUTING WRITERS

Wayne Brouwer is a visiting professor of biblical studies at Hope College and is the author of many books and articles.

Tony Carnes is a senior writer and news reporter for *Christianity Today*. He lives in New York City and specializes in political and urban news coverage.

Noel Castellanos is the founder and president of the Latino Leadership Foundation, and was founding pastor of La Villita Community Church in inner-city Chicago.

Lisa Ann Cockrel is a freelance writer, managing editor for Brazos Press, and a film reviewer for CT Movies (www.christianitytoday.com/movies).

Andy Crouch is editor of the Christian Vision Project (www.christianvisionproject.com) and a coauthor of Emergent's *The Church in Emerging Culture* (Zondervan, 2003).

Mark Galli is managing editor of *Christianity Today* and author of *Jesus Mean and Wild: The Unexpected Love of an Untamable God*, *Francis of Assisi and His World*, and other books.

Edward Gilbreath is director of editorial for Urban Ministries, Inc., editor at large for *Christianity Today*, and the author of *Reconciliation Blues: A Black Evangelical's Inside View of White Christianity*.

Alan Hirsch is an experienced church planter, founding director of Forge Mission Training Network, and the author of *The Forgotten Ways*. You can learn more about Alan and his ministry at www.theforgottenways.org.

Bill Hybels is senior pastor of Willow Creek Community Church in South Barrington, Illinois.

Richard A. Kauffman is a former associate editor of *Christianity Today* and is now senior editor at *The Christian Century*.

John Koessler serves as chair and professor of pastoral studies at Moody Bible Institute. He is the author of several books, including his memoir A *Stranger in the House of God: From Doubt to Faith and Everywhere in Between* (Zondervan).

Joy-Elizabeth Lawrence is a freelance writer who lives with her husband in Grand Rapids, Michigan.

Gordon MacDonald is editor at large of *Leadership* and chair of World Relief and lives in Belmont, New Hampshire.

Scot McKnight is professor of religious studies at North Park Theological Seminary in Chicago, Illinois. He is author of *The Jesus Creed* and he blogs at jesuscreed.org.

Rob Moll is *Christianity Today* Editor at Large.

A. Koshy Muthalaly is a professor at Southern Nazarene University in Bethany, OK.

Brandon O'Brien is assistant editor of *Leadership* and BuildingChurchLeaders.com.

Sam O'Neal is managing editor of the Discipleship Team at Christianity Today International, where he works primarily on producing and editing resources for SmallGroups.com.

Soong-Chan Rah is senior pastor of Cambridge Community Fellowship Church, a multiethnic, urban-ministry-focused church reaching postmoderns in Cambridge, Massachusetts.

JoHannah Reardon is managing editor of ChristianBibleStudies.com.

Frank Reid is senior pastor of the historic Bethel African Methodist Episcopal Church in Baltimore.

Tim Stafford is a senior writer for *Christianity Today* and the author of many books, including *Personal God: Can You Really Know the One Who Made the Universe?* (Zondervan).

John Stott is a pastor, respected evangelical leader, and prolific author. You can learn more about his current work with the Langham Partnership at www.johnstottministries.org.

Agnieszka Tennant was an editor at large for *Christianity Today*. She is now pursuing graduate studies at Northwestern University.

Kelli B. Trujillo is an editor, author, and adult ministry leader at her church in Indianapolis.

Kyle White is the founding director of Neighbors' House, a ministry to at-risk students in DeKalb, Illinois. He is a freelance writer and blogs at kyleLwhite.blogspot.com.

INTRODUCTION

What will the future be like? Some immediately think of space hotels on Mars, microchip-sized cell phones, and cars that fly. Others think of tapped-out fossil fuels, political upheaval, and continents scorched by nuclear war.

But how often do we think of *the church*? The future, with all of its promise and all of its potential problems, looms large in front of us; will we move effectively into the future as a vibrant, bright witness to the gospel? Or will the church simply become a cultural relic that's viewed as completely irrelevant to society?

In this study you'll examine some of the issues we must consider as we determine how to strengthen the church to fulfill God's mission in the future. You'll look at cultural issues like postmodernism and the increasing ethnic diversity of society. You'll explore recent trends within the church, like the embrace of orthodoxy among the young, church-planting, and the emerging church movement. And you'll consider how the church can and should respond to future tragedies and disasters that will eclipse events like 9/11.

Ultimately the study series will conclude with you—with your part in committing wholeheartedly to be a part of the church, complete with its flaws and failings. What part will *you* play in the future of the church? This *Current Issues Bible Study* guide is designed to facilitate lively and engaging discussion on various facets of this topic and how it connects to our lives as Jesus's followers. As you explore the topic of the church's future together, we hope this *Current Issues Bible Study* guide will help you grow closer as a group and challenge you in ways you may not expect.

For Small Groups

These studies are designed to be used in small groups—communities of people with a commitment to and connection with each other. Whether you're an existing small group or you're just planning to meet for the next eight weeks, this resource will help you deepen your personal faith and grow closer with each other.

For additional help, you can go to SmallGroups.com to find everything you need to successfully run a small-groups ministry. The insightful, free articles and theme-specific downloads provide expert training. The reproducible curriculum courses bring thought leaders from across the world into your group's discussion at a fraction of the price. And the revolutionary SmallGroupsConnect social network will help keep your group organized and connected 24/7.

Christianity Today Articles

Each study session begins with one or two thought-provoking articles from *Christianity Today* or one of its sister publications. These articles are meant to help you dive deeply into the topic and engage with a variety of thoughts and opinions. Be sure to read the articles before you arrive to your small group meeting; the time you invest on the front end will greatly enrich your group's discussion. As you read, you may find the articles persuasive and agree heartily with their conclusions; other times you may disagree with the claims of an article, but that's great too. We want these articles to serve as a springboard for lively discussion, so differences in opinion are welcome. For more insightful articles from *Christianity Today* magazine, visit http://www.ctlibrary.com/ and subscribe now.

Timing

These studies are designed to be flexible, with plenty of discussion, activities, and prayer time to fill a full small group meeting. If you'd like, you can zero in on a few questions or teaching points and discuss them in greater depth, or you can aim to spend a few minutes on each question of a given session. Be sure to manage your time so that you're able to spend time on the "Going Forward" questions and prayer time at the end of each study.

Ground Rules

True spiritual growth happens in the context of a vibrant Christian community. To establish that type of community in your small group, we recommend a few *ground rules*.

- *Guarantee confidentiality*. Promise together that whatever is said in the context of your small group meeting is *kept* there. This sense of trust and safety will enable you to more honestly share your spiritual struggles.

- *Participate—with balance*. We all have different personalities. Some of us like to talk . . . a lot. Others of us prefer to be quiet. But for this study to truly benefit your group, everyone needs to participate. Make it a personal goal to answer (aloud) at least half of the discussion questions in a given session. This will allow space for others to talk (lest you dominate discussion too much) but will also guarantee your own contribution is made to the discussion (from which other group members will benefit).

- *Be an attentive listener—to each other and to God*. As you read Scripture and discuss these important cultural issues, focus with care and love on the other members of your group. These questions are designed to be open-ended and to allow for a diversity of opinion. Be gracious toward others who express views that are different than your own. And even more important, prayerfully remain attentive to the presence of God speaking to and guiding your group through the Holy Spirit.

It is our prayer that this *Current Issues Bible Study* will change the lives of your group members as you seek to integrate your faith into the cultural issues you face every day. May the Holy Spirit work in and through your group as you challenge and encourage each other in spiritual growth.

CURRENT ISSUES: THE FUTURE OF THE CHURCH

As our world changes, what should—and shouldn't—change about the church?

Galatians 5:22–25

Ecclesiastes 3:9–14

THE CHURCH IN THE TWENTY-FIRST CENTURY

■

If you attended church as a child, what do you remember about it? Dressing up, women wearing hats, and men removing theirs before entering the building? Did you sing hymns from a hymnal? Sit in wooden pews? What was the sermon like? What about Sunday school? Do you remember flannelgraph stories, the wordless book, songs with hand motions?

If you didn't attend church, did you know friends who did? Were they different from you? Did you ever visit church with a friend? What were your impressions?

In the past hundred years it seems that the church has changed *a lot*. But is this change simply a change of presentation or is it a core transition? And how should we view this change—with sighs of relief or with tremors of trepidation?

■ Before You Meet

Read the interview with John Stott by Tim Stafford entitled "Evangelism Plus: John Stott reflects on where we've been and where we're going."

EVANGELISM PLUS

John Stott reflects on where we've been and where we're going.

Interview by Tim Stafford

In 2004, *New York Times* columnist David Brooks wrote that if evangelicals chose a pope, they would likely select John Stott. Stott, eighty-five, has been at the heart of evangelical renewal in the U.K. His books and biblical sermons have transfixed millions throughout the world. He has been involved in many important world councils and dialogues, not least as chair of the committees that drafted the Lausanne Covenant (1974) and the Manila Manifesto (1989)—two defining statements for evangelicals. For more than thirty-five years, he has devoted three months of every year to traveling the globe, with a particular emphasis on churches in the majority world. He is ideally suited to comment on evangelicals' past, present, and future. CT senior writer Tim Stafford interviewed him at his home in London.

As you see it, what is evangelicalism, and why does it matter?

An evangelical is a plain, ordinary Christian. We stand in the mainstream of historic, orthodox, biblical Christianity. So we can recite the Apostles Creed and the Nicene Creed without crossing our fingers. We believe in God the Father and in Jesus Christ and in the Holy Spirit.

Having said that, there are two particular things we like to emphasize: the concern for authority on the one hand and salvation on the other.

For evangelical people, our authority is the God who has spoken supremely in Jesus Christ. And that is equally true of redemption or salvation. God has acted in and through Jesus Christ for the salvation of sinners.

I think it's necessary for evangelicals to add that what God has said in Christ and in the biblical witness to Christ, and what God has *done* in and through Christ, are both, to use the Greek word, *hapax*—meaning once and for all. There is a finality about God's word in Christ, and there is a finality about God's work in Christ. To imagine that we could add a word to his word, or add a work to his work, is extremely derogatory to the unique glory of our Lord Jesus Christ.

You didn't mention the Bible, which would surprise some people.

I did, actually, but you didn't notice it. I said Christ and the biblical witness to Christ. But the really distinctive emphasis is on Christ. I want to shift conviction from a book, if you like, to a person. As Jesus himself said, the Scriptures bear witness to me. Their main function is to witness to Christ.

Part of your implication is that evangelicals are not to be a negatively inspired people. Our real focus ought to be the glory of Christ.

I believe that very strongly. We believe in the authority of the Bible because Christ has endorsed its authority. He stands between the two testaments. As we look back to the Old Testament, he has endorsed it. As we look forward to the New Testament, we accept it because of the apostolic witness to Christ. He deliberately chose and appointed and prepared the apostles, in order that they might have their unique apostolic witness to him.

How has the position of evangelicals changed during your years of ministry?

I look back—it's been sixty-one years since I was ordained—and when I was ordained in the Church of England, evangelicals in the Church of England were a despised and rejected minority. The bishops lost no opportunity to ridicule us. Over the intervening sixty years, I've seen the evangelical movement in England grow in size, in maturity, certainly in scholarship, and therefore I think in influence and impact.

We went from a ghetto to being on the ascendancy, which is a very dangerous place to be.

Can you comment on the dangers?
Pride is the ever-present danger that faces all of us. In many ways, it is good for us to be despised and rejected. I think of Jesus's words, "Woe unto you when all men speak well of you."

Going back to the *hapax*, it's a very humbling concept. The essence of evangelicalism is very humbling. You have William Temple saying, "The only thing of my very own which I contribute to redemption is the sin from which I need to be redeemed."

We have also seen an immense growth of the church worldwide, largely along evangelical lines. What do you see as its significance?
This enormous growth is a fulfillment of God's promise to Abraham in Genesis 12:1–4. God promised Abraham not only to bless him, not only to bless his family or his posterity, but through his posterity to bless all the families of the earth. Whenever we look at a multiethnic congregation, we are seeing a fulfillment of that amazing promise of God. A promise made by God to Abraham four thousand years ago is being fulfilled right before our very eyes today.

You know this growing church probably as well as any Westerner does. I wonder how you evaluate it.
The answer is "growth without depth." None of us wants to dispute the extraordinary growth of the church. But it has been largely numerical and statistical growth. And there has not been sufficient growth in discipleship that is comparable to the growth in numbers.

How can the Western church, which surely has problems of its own, fruitfully interact with the non-Western? Right now many churches are sending mission teams all over the world.
I certainly want to be positive about short-term mission trips, and I think on the whole they are a good thing. They do give Westerners an

awfully good opportunity to taste Southern Christianity and to be challenged by it, especially by its exuberant vitality. But I think the leaders of such mission trips would be wise to warn their members that this is only a very limited experience of cross-cultural mission.

True mission that is based on the example of Jesus involves entering another world, the world of another culture. Incarnational cross-cultural mission is and can be very costly. I want to say, please realize that if God calls you to be a cross-cultural missionary, it will take you ten years to learn the language and to learn the culture in such a way that you are accepted more or less as a national.

So there's really no replacing the long-term missionary.
I think not, except of course for indigenous Christians.

What about what some call the greatest mission field, which is our own secularizing or secularized culture? What do we need to do to reach this increasingly pagan society?
I think we need to say to one another that it's not so secular as it looks. I believe that these so-called secular people are engaged in a quest for at least three things. The first is transcendence. It's interesting in a so-called secular culture how many people are looking for something beyond. I find that a great challenge to the quality of our Christian worship. Does it offer people what they are instinctively looking for, which is transcendence, the reality of God?

The second is significance. Almost everybody is looking for his or her own personal identity. Who am I, where do I come from, where am I going to, what is it all about? That is a challenge to the quality of our Christian teaching. We need to teach people who they are. They don't know who they are. We do. They are human beings made in the image of God, although that image has been defaced.

And third is their quest for community. Everywhere, people are looking for community, for relationships of love. This is a challenge to our fellowship. I'm very fond of 1 John 4:12: "No one has ever seen God; if we love one another, God abides in us, and his love is perfected in us." The invisibility of God is a great problem to people.

The same invisible God who once made himself visible in Jesus now makes himself visible in the Christian community, *if we love one another*. And all the verbal proclamation of the gospel is of little value unless it is made by a community of love.

These three things about our humanity are on our side in our evangelism, because people are looking for the very things we have to offer them.

And therefore you're not despairing of the West.

I'm not despairing. But I believe that evangelism is specially through the local church, through the community, rather than through the individual. That the church should be an alternative society, a visible sign of the kingdom. And the tragedy is that our local churches often don't seem to manifest community.

Biblical preaching has fallen on hard times in many places. What do you say to a pastor who is desperately trying to hold his congregation's attention and really doesn't have the confidence that enables one to just preach from a biblical text?

It's the same issue across the globe. Churches live, grow, and flourish by the Word of God. And they languish and even perish without it.

So the Langham Partnership International has three basic convictions. Conviction one is that God wants his church to grow. One of the verses that expresses this best is Colossians 1:28–29, in which Paul says we proclaim Christ, warning everybody and teaching everybody in all wisdom, in order that we may present everybody mature in Christ. There's a plain call to maturity, to grow up out of babyhood.

Second, they grow by the Word of God. I suppose you could concede that there are other ways by which the church grows, but if you take the New Testament as a whole, it's the Word of God that matures the people of God.

Which brings me to the third conviction, that the Word of God comes to the people of God mainly, though not exclusively, through preaching. I often envisage on a Sunday morning the amazing spectacle of the people of God converging on their places of worship all over the world. They're going to medieval cathedrals, to house churches, to the open air. They know that in the course of the worship service there will be a sermon, and it should be a biblical sermon, so that through the Word of God they may grow.

When I enter the pulpit with the Bible in my hands and in my heart, my blood begins to flow and my eyes to sparkle for the sheer glory of having God's Word to expound. We need to emphasize the glory, the privilege, of sharing God's truth with people.

Where do we evangelicals need to go? We've been through quite a trip in the last fifty years.

My immediate answer is that we need to go beyond evangelism. Evangelism is supposed to be evangelicals' specialty. Now, I am totally committed to world evangelization. But we must look beyond evangelism to the transforming power of the gospel, both in individuals and in society.

With regard to individuals, I'm noting in different expressions of the evangelical faith an absence of that quest for holiness that marked our forebears. Somehow *holiness* has a rather sanctimonious feel to it. People don't like to be described as holy. But the holiness of the New Testament is Christlikeness. I wish that the whole evangelical movement could consciously set before us the desire to grow in Christlikeness such as is described in Galatians 5:22–23.

Regarding social transformation, I've reflected a great deal on the salt and light metaphors, the models that Jesus himself chose in Matthew 5 in the Sermon on the Mount. "You are the salt of the earth; you are the light of the world." It seems to me that those models must be said to contain at least three things.

First, that Christians are radically different from non-Christians, or if they are not, they ought to be. Jesus sets over against each other two communities. On the one hand there is the world, and on the other hand there is you, who are the dark world's light. Jesus implied that we are as different as light from darkness and salt from decay.

Second, Christians must permeate non-Christian society. Salt does no good if it stays in the saltshaker. Light does no good if you hide it under a bed or bucket. It has to permeate the darkness. So both metaphors call us, not just to be different, but to permeate society.

The third, the more controversial implication, is that the salt and light metaphors indicate that Christians can change non-Christian society. The models must mean that, because both salt and light are effective commodities. They change the environments in which they are placed. Salt hinders bacterial decay. Light dispels darkness. This is not to resurrect the social gospel. We cannot perfect society. But we can improve it.

My hope is that in the future, evangelical leaders will ensure that their social agenda includes such vital but controversial topics as halting climate change, eradicating poverty, abolishing armories of mass destruction, responding adequately to the AIDS pandemic, and asserting the human rights of women and children in all cultures. I hope our agenda does not remain too narrow.

John Stott is a pastor, respected evangelical leader, and prolific author. You can learn more about his current work with the Langham Partnership at www.johnstottministries.org. Tim Stafford is a senior writer for Christianity Today *and the author of many books, including* Personal God: Can You Really Know the One Who Made the Universe? *(Zondervan). "Evangelism Plus" was first published in* Christianity Today, *October 2006.*

■ Open Up

Select one of the following options to begin your discussion today.

Option 1

Give everyone an opportunity to answer at least one of the following icebreaker questions:

- What do you miss most about "the way church used to be"?
- What do you miss the least?
- What do you appreciate most about the contemporary church?
- What bothers you the most?

Option 2

Each person should bring two to four "artifacts" from previous decades. Artifacts could include photographs of cars or clothing styles, vintage clothing, records or cassette tapes, old magazines, or any other household items your own.

Write out on index cards these decades: 1940s or earlier, 1950s, 1960s, 1970s, 1980s, 1990s, and 2000s.

Now set out the index cards in one area and the artifacts in another. Work together to place the artifacts near the decade that best fits them.

Look at the various artifacts together and reminisce about those decades (if you were alive then). If you attended church during any of those decades, share your memories and stories with each other. What was church like at that time? How is it like or unlike the church you attend today?

■ The Issue

- As you look ahead to the next fifty years, what changes and challenges do you think are on the horizon for the church? Why?

There's no doubt about it: the church changed in the twentieth century and it will continue to change in the twenty-first century.

- Did this article lead you to hope or despair? Why?

■ Reflect

Read Ecclesiastes 3:9–14 and Galatians 5:22–25 on your own. Take a few moments to meditate quietly on these passages, then jot down some notes about what you observe. What stands out to you from these passages? How might they relate to the church today or the culture today?

■ Let's Explore

The Church in a Postmodern World

Gordon MacDonald, in his book *Who Stole My Church,* has a fictional pastor explain "postmodernism" as follows:

> Postmodernism begins with the idea that there are no fixed, stand-alone truths. Rather than this thing called truth coming from beyond ourselves—as Christians believe about God's revelation—the postmodernist claims that truth is really only what *we* see or experience from our perspective.

- How does this compare or contrast with your understanding of postmodernism?

- Why is postmodernism perceived by some to work against Christianity? Do you agree with this perspective? Or do you think postmodernism can benefit Christianity? Explain.

SESSION 1: THE CHURCH IN THE TWENTY-FIRST CENTURY

John Stott mentioned three things that "so-called secular people are engaged in a quest for." These three things were transcendence, significance, and community.

- How have you seen examples of these quests in our culture or in the lives of people you know? Share specific examples of the quest for transcendence, the quest for significance, and the quest for community.

Read Ecclesiastes 3:9–14. (If you have time, also read Ecclesiastes 2:1–26.)

- How does this passage from Ecclesiastes speak to these spiritual quests? How have you observed the truth of this passage in the lives of people you know?

- Do you think these are these "modern" or "postmodern" quests? How have you seen the church responding to them? Or in what ways *should* the church respond to them?

- How does a postmodern worldview coincide with the idea that God has set "eternity in the hearts" of humanity?

The Church Amid a Spiritual Revival

In the book *Who Stole My Church?* the pastor suggests that there's a revival happening, saying, "People are finding it easier to talk about spirituality, about evil, about powers and believing." And John Stott commented that our secular culture "is not so secular as it looks."

- Do you agree that there may be a revival happening in our culture? If so, have you witnessed this revival? What examples have you seen? If not, why do you disagree?

- Do you feel the church is adequately responding to this revival? What sort of answer is the church providing for "postmodern/spiritual" people?

Read Galatians 5:22–25.

- How can the fruit of the Spirit aid us in responding to this spiritual revival? Give real-life examples, if you have them.

- Usually we think of the fruits of the Spirit as attributes expressed in individual people. But perhaps we should also look for them as evidence of God's work within the church as a whole. How is the church today characterized by the fruit of the Spirit? In what particular fruits do you think the church is lacking?

SESSION 1: THE CHURCH IN THE TWENTY-FIRST CENTURY

The Church's Transforming Power

John Stott challenges us by saying, "I am totally committed to world evangelization. But we must look beyond evangelism to the transforming power of the gospel, both in individuals and in society."

- What are historical or personal examples you can share of how the gospel is transformational within a society?

- Have you seen evidence of fruits of the Spirit in today's society? Where?

- What are ways we can "follow the Spirit" while the church undergoes great change?

- What do you think is the great challenge facing the church in the twenty-first century based upon your experience and Stott's interview?

■ Going Forward

- In what ways do you think the church needs to change as the culture around us changes? In what ways shouldn't the church change?

- What is the difference between preferences and truth-essentials when discussing church change? How do you discern between the two?

Pair up with another person in your group and discuss the challenges we each face as our churches change and grow. Select one of the following action steps that will best respond to your concern and talk about it with your partner.

1. If you struggle with a bad attitude toward changes within the church, decide to pray and commit your attitude about the church to God everyday.
2. If you find yourself arguing over small issues with other Christians, commit yourself to finding subjects of consonance with other Christians, so that you may build each other up and find agreement in your belief in the work of Christ.
3. Consider visiting another local church in order to experience different types of worship and perspectives of evangelism.

Write out a prayer that focuses on God's continued work in his church. Pray it together with your partner and then continue to pray it everyday for the next week.

SESSION 1: THE CHURCH IN THE TWENTY-FIRST CENTURY

■ Notes

CURRENT ISSUES: THE FUTURE OF THE CHURCH

Is church planting the new (old) wave of evangelism?

John 1:1–18

Acts 2:42–47

PLANT A CHURCH, MAKE A CONVERT

■

We've seen it all, haven't we? Evangelistic magicians. Evangelistic clowns. Evangelistic muscle men. Even, evangelistic "horse whisperers"! Whatever we think of them, they presumably operate from a genuine motivation of trying to creatively reach our ever-changing culture with the good news of the kingdom.

We all struggle with that dilemma. We know that we can't become stagnant in our outreach; there must be new wineskins for new wine, right (Matthew 9:15)? So, wouldn't it be interesting if the new wineskin for evangelism today was the retro-wineskin of church planting? The church-planting trend is growing quickly—is this movement the new cutting edge of evangelism? Why are church plants so effective today in reaching the lost? And will this method continue to be effective in the future as our culture continues to change?

■ Before You Meet

Read "Go and Plant Churches of All Peoples" from *Christianity Today* magazine.

GO AND PLANT CHURCHES OF ALL PEOPLES

Crusades and personal witnessing are no longer
the cutting edge of evangelism.

by Tim Stafford

Fifty years ago, if you said *evangelism* in a word-association game, you would probably get back *Billy Graham*. Crusade evangelism dominated the American church's ideas about reaching out. When First Baptist Church members decided to share the gospel with their neighbors, they looked to see which evangelist could come to town.

Thirty years ago, crusades began to wane, and personal evangelism came to dominate our thoughts. A church that wanted to reach out would typically offer a class on how to use the "Four Spiritual Laws" or Evangelism Explosion to witness to friends and strangers.

Crusades haven't disappeared, and churches still teach personal witness. But today, church planting is the default mode for evangelism. Go to any evangelical denomination, ask them what they are doing to grow, and they will refer you to the church-planting office. I have talked to Southern Baptists, General Conference Baptists, the Evangelical Free Church, the Assemblies of God, the Foursquare Church, the Acts 29 network, and a variety of independent practitioners and observers. I quit going to more because they all said the same thing: "We're excited and committed to church planting. It's the cutting edge."

Many Motivations

Frustration with other methodologies has something to do with this trend. Despite many tales of triumph and huge resources mobilized—think of the "Here's Life, America" campaign—it's hard to trace an overall difference. "North America is the only continent in the world where the church is not growing," says Eric Ramsey of the Southern Baptist Convention's North American Mission Board (NAMB).

Biblical rethinking also fuels the conviction that church planting is the ideal way to fulfill Jesus's Great Commission. "It's apparent in the Great Commission that we are to make disciples through the avenue of churches," says Scott Thomas of the Acts 29 Network, a church-planting organization affiliated with Seattle's Mars Hill Church. "The whole Book of Acts offers that model."

Acts 29 churches view planting as essential to the nature of the church. They expect that at least 10 percent of every offering—including a church's first offering—will go toward church planting. They join an increasing number of church leaders who see Western individualism as sub-Christian. Aren't disciples made in the context of community?

Perhaps most important, studies show a consistent difference between old and new churches. George Hunter of Asbury Theological Seminary says, "Churches after fifteen years typically plateau. After thirty-five years, they typically can't even replace those [members] they lose. New congregations reach a lot more pre-Christian people." Those who study churches say established congregations tend to turn inward, no matter how hard they try to resist the trend. But new churches must look outward to survive. Richard Harris, vice president of NAMB's church-planting group, says that established SBC churches report 3.4 baptisms per 100 resident members, whereas new churches average 11.7. It's not hard to conclude that more new churches would lead more people to Christ.

Gary Rohrmayer, director of church planting for the Midwest Baptist Conference, told me of a 1,200-member church that planted a church. The new church quickly grew to two hundred, but in the same time period, the 1,200-member church grew to 1,600. Seeing that the established church had actually added more members, leaders wondered whether they should put their resources into expanding their own ministry instead of planting another church. When asked how many adult converts they had seen in that period, however, they named eight. The new church had about one hundred. "You [tell] me whether you should start another church or not," Rohrmayer says.

Tough Calling

No denomination invests more in church planting than the Southern Baptist Convention. America's largest Protestant body wants to double its number of congregations in the next twenty years, to one hundred thousand. Richard Harris says they have been starting four churches a day, but they need to increase that number to eight or ten.

These are not your father's Southern Baptist churches. I attended an "opportunity tour" in San Francisco's East Bay. Upwards of sixty church leaders from throughout the country boarded vans to see where the East Bay Baptist Association needed help starting churches. My tour began in the Canal District of San Rafael, where a recent seminary graduate, Marian Engelland, is trying to establish a church among Guatemalan immigrants in low-income apartments. From there we hopped across the bay to San Pablo, where a African American preacher named Port Wilburn leads a team trying to re-launch a struggling inner-city church and re-envision it to reach a new middle-class housing development. Then we had lunch with eighteen Chinese pastors in Oakland's Chinatown, where the SBC wants to start a church among restaurant workers who typically work Sunday mornings and need to meet late at night. Finally, we traveled to Fremont, where another recent seminary graduate reaches out to the sixty thousand Afghan immigrants in the area.

Sixty percent of the SBC's new churches focus on ethnic minorities. "They are quite cutting edge," Wheaton College's Scott Moreau says of SBC church planters. "You can plant a church that looks like a mosque." Still, other East Bay tours looked at plans to start churches in elite Anglo neighborhoods and one aiming to become a regional seeker-sensitive church at Jack London Square, a cultural gathering spot near downtown Oakland.

Lyman Alexander, the East Bay's director of missions, says they hope to add ten new churches a year and double the East Bay association. "Money is the biggest hindrance, because it is so expensive to live here," Alexander says. "People come and look at the cost of living, and they say, 'I'll starve.' God definitely has to call them here."

Niche Audiences

In years past, evangelism didn't necessarily motivate church planting. Southern Baptists, for example, planted churches as they moved out of the South, taking the comforts of home with them. Methodists started churches in the suburbs that attracted their upwardly mobile church members who migrated out of the inner city. Such churches still get planted, but their number has declined along with denominational loyalty.

Today's church plants often target immigrants, which means adjusting church traditions to diverse ethnic cultures. "Any denomination that has an aggressive church-planting program and doesn't have a bias toward the white community will be largely ethnic," says David Ripley, who leads ethnic ministries at the Billy Graham Center in Wheaton, Illinois. "If we are challenging people to reach their neighbors, the reality is that the neighborhood is changing." As an example, he notes that twenty-five languages are spoken at Wheaton North High School, formerly dominated by WASP students.

So-called emerging churches also plant churches, since the kind of ministry they espouse doesn't exist in traditional bodies. "Looking at churches today, are they likely to reach the next generation for Christ?" asks Eddie Gibbs of Fuller Theological Seminary. "So many of our churches are the product of Christendom: open the door and let them come in."

Many emerging churches prefer the term *missional*, and though it's a hard term to pin down precisely, its affinity with *missionary* captures an adventurous, unconventional, and non-institutional spirit that focuses outward. Their audience may be largely Anglo, but it knows as little about Christianity as Thai Buddhist immigrants.

Church plants also frequently arise out of the seeker-sensitive models pioneered by churches like Willow Creek Community Church in South Barrington, Illinois. "When they say they are reaching the unchurched, often they are reaching the de-churched," Gibbs says. Many Americans have family memories of church as an important place for spiritual development and comfort, but they have lost their connection to it. Church plants can offer a smaller, more relational, or less conventional approach that lures them back. Church planters may refer to this as an "attractional" ministry, as distinct from missional.

Insights from Overseas

So church planting actually involves quite different strategies for evangelism: immigrant, missional, and attractional, for a start. Some are launched by pioneer missionaries, sent out into new territory or toward a new target group. Others grow from cuttings. A team of one hundred or more deliberately leave a mother church to start a new one. Sometimes, large churches start satellite operations that gradually grow independent. Or multiple congregations inhabit the same building, reaching out to different audiences. The many strategies help church planters reach diverse audiences, from Cambodian immigrants to latte-sipping, rap-listening hipsters in a Southern California beach community.

Church planters in all these environments see America as a mission field. The missionary surge that took the gospel from America and Europe to Africa, Asia, and South America is now washing back over the West. Lesslie Newbigin predicted it decades ago. On returning to England from a lifetime of missions in India, he wrote that the greatest missionary challenge in the world was the West.

Church-planting insights learned on the mission field have penetrated American church leaders, partly because they know how churches in the developing world have grown. Success-oriented Americans love to hear stories from Africa and China. Developing-world churches, once treated with patriarchal condescension, have a new status. Missionary thinking has a new status too.

Church planting is a missionary approach, typical of the apostle Paul and of most missionaries since. Where there is no church, you have to plant a church. You have to find ways to penetrate the culture with the gospel, and then you have to provide a secure place for disciples to grow and to explore their new identity. A short while ago, we didn't think this way in North America. Now we do.

Furthermore, missionaries become attuned to social barriers that keep the gospel from reaching everybody—barriers of religion, language,

SESSION 2: PLANT A CHURCH, MAKE A CONVERT

tribe, caste, and socioeconomic status. A church may thrive among one group and miss a neighboring group entirely. You have to target each group separately, or you won't reach everybody. Missionaries who go overseas learn to think sociologically because they stand outside the culture looking in. That same sociological perspective has penetrated church planting at home.

Planters Persevere

Despite what some say, the United States is not a post-Christian nation. It's more half Christian and half post-Christian, trying to make up its mind. A sizeable share of Americans describe themselves as Bible-believing Christians. In many places and contexts you can still reach people simply by opening the doors and offering a worship service.

That's missions. It is not easy. Many first-term missionaries give up and go home. Only the entrepreneurial, independent, and stubborn personalities who want so badly to plant churches stick with it. Nonetheless, a church that seeks to obey the Great Commission will keep sending out missionaries. And missionaries plant churches—even when they never leave home.

Tim Stafford is a senior writer for Christianity Today *and the author of many books, including* Personal God: Can You Really Know the One Who Made the Universe? *(Zondervan). "Go and Plant Churches of All Peoples" was first published in* Christianity Today, *September 27, 2007.*

■ Open Up

Select one of these activities to launch your discussion time.

Option 1

Discuss these icebreaker questions:

- What immediately comes to mind for you when you hear the word *evangelism*? A person? An event? A feeling? Explain.

- When have you seen churches get evangelism "right"? When have you seen them get it wrong?

Option 2

Split your study group in half. One team should work together to create a list entitled "The Top 10 Worst Evangelism Ideas." These can be real evangelism methods they've heard about or could be completely made up.

The other team should work together to create a list entitled "The Top 10 Evangelism Ideas for the Year 2025." This team should come up with both funny and serious evangelism ideas for the church of the future.

After about five minutes, teams should gather back together. Share your lists with each other, then talk about these questions:

- How have you seen evangelism methods change over the years since you've been a Christian?
- When have you had a memorable experience with evangelism? Is it memorable because it was a positive experience or a negative experience? Explain.

■ The Issue

- Does it bother you that we seem to be always striving for "cutting edge" (the article uses this phrase several times) evangelism? Should evangelism change? Should we continue to invent and try out various evangelism methods and models? Why or why not?

Tim Stafford's *Christianity Today* article, "Go and Plant Churches of All Peoples," reports that, "[Evangelistic] crusades haven't disappeared, and churches still teach personal witness. But today, church planting is the default mode. Go to any evangelical denomination, ask them what they are doing to grow, and they will refer you to the church-planting office." This comes in part from a back-to-basics look at Scripture where the "whole book of Acts offers that model."

- Has your church planted other churches? If so, what was the motivation? If not, what would have to happen before your church would make that move?

- Why do you think church planting is such an effective evangelism "method" in today's culture? Do you think it will continue to be effective in the future? Why or why not?

■ Reflect

Read John 1:1–18 and Acts 2:42–47 on your own. Take a few moments to jot down notes and observations. What do they have to say to the church? Is there any link between these passages? What questions do you have after reading them?

■ Let's Explore

Churches must reflect the good news of God's kingdom.

It's been said that the church is like Noah's ark; if it wasn't for the storm on the outside, you wouldn't be able stand the smell on the inside. Yikes! Although there may be some truth here, Scripture calls the church to much more. It is the vehicle for the gospel and thus must reflect the values of God's kingdom; not just through talk but through action and atmosphere as well. Imagine how attractive that would be to unbelievers in our communities.

- What does Acts 2:42–47 tell you about Christ and his power? About the values of his kingdom?

- Why do you think people were being saved daily (v. 47)?

Stafford quotes George Hunter of Asbury Seminary: "Churches after fifteen years typically plateau. After thirty-five years, they can't even replace those [members] they lose. New congregations reach a lot more pre-Christian people." Where older churches become ingrown and focused on self-maintenance, church plants naturally focus outward and can minister to the niches of ethnicity, social class, and culture.

- What has been the ebb and flow of your church's evangelism as your church has become more established in your community? Has evangelism increased or has the focus become more inward? Why?

- Make a list of all the actions of the new church as it is described in Acts 2. What are the characteristics of this new body of believers?

- In what ways does this passage describe *your* church? In what ways does your church *not* reflect this early picture of Christian community?

Churches must always move into others' worlds with the Good News of God's kingdom.

Whether we think church planting is the "cutting edge" of evangelism or not, we cannot ignore Christ's command to *"go* and make disciples" (Matthew 28:19, NIV). The *going* is explicit. But before Jesus commanded us to "go," he modeled it for us.

- What does John 1:1–18 tell you about God? About Jesus, the Word? What is the Word's mission?

- How does it affect you that "the Word became a human" for our sake? For *your* sake?

Verse 14 says he "lived among us" or "made his dwelling among us" (NIV). The word for dwelling is "tabernacled." Essentially, Jesus, in his Incarnation, "pitched his tent" with us in our world of need. Eugene Peterson renders it this way in *The Message*: "He moved into our neighborhood."

- What is the ministry/evangelism model here for us? What could "incarnational ministry" look like in your community through your church?

- Does your church live "in the neighborhood" of your community? In other words, does it connect well with the people groups in your area? The issues? The needs? Explain.

■ Going Forward

Eddie Gibbs of Fuller Seminary asks, "Looking at churches today, are they likely to reach the next generation for Christ?"

- What's your opinion? How do you think the church—your church—would need to change to reach the *next* generation?

Gibbs goes on to say, "Many of our churches are the product of Christendom: open the door and let them come in."

SESSION 2: PLANT A CHURCH, MAKE A CONVERT

- In what new ways could you/your small group or church more actively move out into the community rather than asking people to come to you? Brainstorm specific ideas.

- Do you and your church need to plant a church? Why or why not? Look at your community. Where would you plant a church? What social barriers have not been scaled for the gospel? What can you, your small group, or your church do to overcome those even now?

- One of the church planting networks in the article is called Acts 29 Network. There are only twenty-eight chapters in Acts. How is your church writing the next chapter of Acts?

As a group, pray for your goals in these areas. Recommit together to reflecting God's kingdom values in your church and to going into the world with the good news of the kingdom.

CURRENT ISSUES: THE FUTURE OF THE CHURCH

Do the traditions of the past make for a healthy church of the future—or do they breed an empty faith?

Mark 7:1–8

Colossians 2:6–10, 20–23

2 Peter 1:16–21

SESSION 3

TRADITION: LOVE IT OR LOSE IT?

■

Some Evangelicals have a tendency to disparage tradition—to associate it with dead orthodoxy, a fire extinguisher that quenches the work of the Spirit. Yet other evangelicals—particularly the young—are returning to traditional practices drawn from church history with great fervor. They look to the past to help them define the church of the future.

In "The Tradition Temptation," Roger Olson points out that part of growing as disciples of Jesus is to learn the language and practices of the faith from generations past; we don't start from scratch as Christians, and each new generation doesn't create a new way of being Christian.

In this study we will explore what Jesus taught about tradition and learn how we can find the right place for tradition in our faith.

■ Before You Meet

Read "The Tradition Temptation" from *Christianity Today*.

THE TRADITION TEMPTATION

Why we should still give Scripture pride of place.

by Roger E. Olson

Like Many Evangelicals, I grew up in a church that objected to "tradition," which we associated with dead orthodoxy. A furor erupted in the church office when the new, young associate pastor suggested that the Sunday worship folder contain a minimal order of worship. We disdained formality and embraced the spontaneity of the Spirit in worship. Or so we liked to think. The associate pastor's suggestion was rejected on the ground that printed orders of worship led to liturgy and liturgy was tradition. Some in the congregation whispered that the associate pastor was losing his zeal by attending seminary. The young minister yielded, but he pointed out that he was giving in to *their tradition* of rejecting liturgy and embracing informal, unplanned worship. He also said that since our worship services were pretty routine, we should help visitors by printing our normal order and then allow the Spirit to move within it.

The associate pastor's argument didn't sway the congregation, but it planted new thoughts about tradition in my mind. Had we developed our own traditions, including a tradition of rejecting whatever we perceived as the traditions of other churches that were not "full gospel" (as we called our type of church)?

Like the church I grew up in, numerous evangelical churches like to think that tradition is a Spirit-quenching fire extinguisher. But the matter of tradition is more complex than my home church imagined at the time, and I have come to appreciate much of the tradition handed on to us from the church's past. Nevertheless, I am troubled and remain concerned when evangelicals start touting "tradition" as a way forward in our faith, as many are doing today.

Memory Loss

Let me be fair: I recognize that a completely traditionless Christianity creates more problems than it solves for the church. Evangelical suspicion of tradition and a yearning to live simply by the Bible go back to the Reformation. But especially in America after the Great Awakenings, a profound distrust of everything "traditional" set in. Many evangelicals now use *tradition* as shorthand for "having the form of religion but denying the power thereof."

Evangelicals have lost their memory of the Great Tradition of Christianity before the rise of revivalism and their own free church (less emphasis on creeds and liturgy) movements. We are like people who have forgotten our family tree and our cultural past—rootless wanderers without landmarks from our past to guide us. Is it any wonder, then, that so much of our preaching and teaching is shallow and that we keep repeating the errors of the past? New forms of the heresies that bedeviled the churches in the generations immediately after the apostles' deaths repeatedly appear in evangelical circles. Too many evangelicals accommodate to the therapeutic mindset of the culture and reduce proclamation to self-help tips. Christianity becomes compatible with too much and loses its cognitive shape. Evangelicalism is in danger of being reduced to a folk religion with little or nothing to say to the world out of its great intellectual heritage.

There is now a new Protestant attention to tradition that holds great promise for renewal of authentic Christianity in churches weakened by doctrinal pluralism and cultural accommodation. United Methodist theologians Thomas Oden and William Abraham, among other mainline Protestant conservatives, herald a revival in the Protestant mainstream through drinking deeply at the wells of the church fathers, through faithful adherence to the early creeds and through submitting to the received declarations of the undivided church's ecumenical councils.

Baptist theologian Daniel H. Williams encourages both mainline and evangelical Protestants to experience church renewal through rediscovering the ancient Christian tradition. Episcopalian Robert Webber appealed to postmoderns to rediscover Christian community across time and space in the ancient orthodoxy of the church fathers. Evangelical

Episcopalian theologian Christopher Hall urges evangelicals to read the Bible and learn theology with the church fathers and avoid the heretical novelties foreign to the church fathers' apprehension of the apostolic testimony.

This new Protestant traditionalism is attractive. What is one to do when people calling themselves Christians deny foundational Christian beliefs such as the Trinity and the two natures of Jesus Christ under the banner of "new light from Scripture"? The church fathers faced a similar situation with heretics who claimed to prove their heresies from Scripture. Not every interpretation of Scripture is equal; some are unreasonable and some are opposed to what the church has always believed. Such are always to be suspected of serious error.

All of this is understandable and laudable. Traditionalism in any form is preferable to the unfettered theological experimentation characteristic of so many mainline Protestant seminaries and denominational bureaucracies, as well as to shallow evangelical experientialism too often found in free church congregations and organizations.

Tradition as an -*ism*

And yet there is a danger almost as great as lost memory, and that is hardening of the categories—traditionalism. Historian Jaroslav Pelikan quipped that "tradition is the living faith of the dead while traditionalism is the dead faith of the living." In theology, however, *traditionalism* has a different connotation. It is the method of theology that treats tradition as an authoritative source and norm for Christian belief and practice alongside or over Scripture itself. Against Roman Catholic traditionalism, the Protestant reformers declared themselves in favor of "Scripture alone" (*sola scriptura*). Many people have misinterpreted this as meaning that Christians should pay no attention to any source other than the Bible, but in fact Luther and Calvin made extensive use of the church fathers in their expositions of Scripture and in their programs for reforming the church. What *sola scriptura* really means is not "Scripture alone" but "Scripture above all." "Scripture first" (*prima scriptura*) would be a better motto for the Protestant view of Scripture as the ultimate source and norm for Christian faith and practice. Traditionalism, however, rejects even *prima scriptura* in favor of an equality or interdependency of Scripture and tradition.

Eastern Orthodox churches make this appeal to the authority of tradition explicit. For them, the church's Great Tradition (as distinct from particular traditions of folk piety) is the grand source and norm, and Scripture is part of that Great Tradition. Roman Catholic traditionalism has a more dynamic view of the Great Tradition. For it, tradition grows as the church faces new issues, though for Catholics the Great Tradition does not include novelties. Every addition is thought to recognize an old truth in a new way. Both Orthodox and Catholic traditionalists believe there are essential beliefs that are not explicitly taught in Scripture. These traditionalists recognize the results of universal councils and some common beliefs of the people of God as essential Christian beliefs, even if they are not directly supported by Scripture. For example, Orthodox tradition includes the veneration of icons as necessary for full Christian worship and devotional life, and Roman Catholic tradition includes belief in the dogmas of Mary's immaculate conception and bodily assumption into heaven.

Protestants have historically considered beliefs and practices not directly supported by Scripture as at best optional and often wrong. Scripture is the sole, supreme source and norm of all Christian belief and practice, and tradition is to be judged by it. That is part of evangelical faith for three reasons: because Jesus contradicted tradition but never Scripture, because it is a basic Protestant principle based on the Reformation experience, and because it is important for the continuing prophetic reform of the church. Evangelicals agree with Protestants generally that the church must be "reformed and always reforming." Treating extra-canonical expressions of truth as equal with Scripture impedes continuing reform. History reveals that the church in all its humanity often needs to be held accountable to a higher standard; Scripture is that standard.

Lately, however, in response to evangelical and mainline forgetfulness of the Great Tradition of Christianity, some evangelicals have been succumbing to a form of traditionalism. Rarely does this take the form of explicit repudiation of *sola scriptura*; instead it often appears in claims that the ancient, ecumenical consensus of the church fathers, creeds and councils, the early church's "rule of faith," or "the apostolic tradition" handed on by the church fathers represents the inviolably authoritative interpretation of Scripture.

The trouble with traditionalism is that it tends to place the theological consensus of the ancient, undivided church (or some interpretation of it) on the same authoritative plane with Scripture and thus undercuts the church's ability to reform itself by appeal to God's Word. In matters of theological development and debate, tradition should get a vote but never a veto, whereas Scripture is the gold standard by which every idea—including those developed within tradition—must be tested. Evangelical traditionalists need to acknowledge more readily than is their tendency that the Holy Spirit is still at work among the faithful people of God, leading them to deeper insights into God's Word that may sometimes correct ancient, medieval, and even Reformation beliefs and practices. Understandably, such an admission raises the specter of a Pandora's box of heretical new readings of Scripture. For all its risks, however, it must not be ruled out. Continuing reform depends on it.

A New Middle Way

What is needed today is a middle way between *sola scriptura* and traditionalism that holds fast to the unique and unsurpassable authority of Scripture even over tradition while requiring respect for the Great Tradition of biblical understanding in the church. The evangelical's stand with regard to Scripture and tradition should be that of Martin Luther, who is supposed to have said, when challenged to recant his "novel" teachings about justification, "Unless I am convinced by Scripture and plain reason—I do not accept the authority of popes and councils, for they have contradicted each other—my conscience is captive to the Word of God. . . . Here I stand, I cannot do otherwise." Luther believed that his rediscovered doctrine of justification by grace through faith alone could not be found in the church fathers or councils. He stated that the church fathers knew little about faith. He even criticized his favorite church father—Augustine—for failing to understand that justification is by faith alone.

Anabaptists and Baptists, of course, must reject traditionalism insofar as it elevates ancient consensus theology to a level alongside Scripture; believers' baptism was not part of the ancient ecumenical consensus, but they are convinced it is required by Scripture and the inner logic of conversion. Nor were the autonomy of the local congregation or the priesthood of all believers part of the ancient Christian consensus. Wesley's doctrine of entire sanctification in a moment is absent from the Great Tradition before him, as is the Calvinist doctrine of limited (particular) atonement.

Yet Luther, the Anabaptists, and Wesley valued the Great Tradition of Christian teaching and stringently resisted the rationalists who wanted to discard the mysterious doctrines of the church's heritage, such as the Trinity and the Incarnation. Luther often quoted the church fathers (even though he disdained some of them). Early Anabaptist leaders such as Balthasar Hubmaier regarded the early church's rule of faith as second only to Scripture in authority. Wesley was fascinated with the Greek fathers and considered them faithful and authoritative interpreters of apostolic Christianity.

Evangelicals, with the Reformers, should view the Great Tradition as dynamic and open to correction and revision in the light of Scripture while valuing the achievements of the early church fathers, the medieval theologians, and the Protestant Reformers.

In the recent debate over the doctrine of God, for example, any departure from so-called classical theism has often been harshly criticized for going against the weight of tradition. There are limits to revising the doctrine of God, and we should respect classical theism and adhere to it where possible, but our evangelical understanding of God's nature and attributes must be determined by Scripture and not by tradition. Many evangelicals are convinced that the philosophical categories have obscured the biblical writers' testimony to God as not only holy, sovereign, transcendent, and free, but also intensely personal, interactive, self-limiting, and vulnerable. This debate must be engaged over Scripture rather than closed with a mere appeal to tradition.

An analogy is the United States Constitution and the history of landmark Supreme Court decisions that serve as precedents for later decisions. Judges and lawyers must know the precedents, but the Constitution is the supreme authority. Landmark decisions of earlier courts can be overturned if they are judged to be inconsistent with the Constitution. No competent judge, however, simply tosses out the history of court decisions. They serve as secondary authorities, guides to interpretation.

So it is with the Bible and the Great Tradition. Evangelicals should study the tradition, for we are not the first to seek answers to difficult questions and problems in theology. However, we must not elevate the tradition to inviolable, authoritative status.

My own study of the Great Tradition of Christian belief led me to see that I have roots deeper than my own church affiliations and deeper than evangelicalism itself. I now want my free church tradition and evangelicalism in general to draw on the deep wells of Orthodox and Catholic Christian thinking, as well as on the wells of Reformation, Puritan, pietist, and revivalist thought. The consensus of Christian belief throughout the ages provides a compass for navigating the often treacherous waters of modern and postmodern religious confusion. It also serves as an anchor when the ship of evangelicalism is prone to drift into market-driven and merely therapeutic preaching. To a large extent, I have Protestant traditionalists to thank for this discovery of the value of the Great Tradition. Nevertheless, we should resist any tendency to pull Scripture down to the level of tradition; the evangelical house of authority must remain solidly on the foundation of *sola (prima) scriptura*. When a new theological idea arises among evangelicals, our first and foremost question must be "What saith the Scriptures?" and not "Is it consistent with tradition?" Like Luther, we must be open to the possibility that the Holy Spirit may break forth new light from Scripture that reforms even the ancient thinking of the church.

Roger E. Olson is a professor of theology at Truett Theological Seminary in Waco, Texas, and author of The Mosaic of Christian Belief: Twenty Centuries of Unity and Diversity *(IVP, 2002). "The Tradition Temptation" was first published in* Christianity Today, *November 2003, Page 52.*

SESSION 3: TRADITION: LOVE IT OR LOSE IT?

■ Open Up

Select one of these activities to launch your discussion time.

Option 1

Discuss these icebreaker questions:

- Think about your personality for a moment: Do you most enjoy thinking about the past (recalling special memories), focusing on the present (being "in the moment"), or pondering the future (dreaming and planning)? In other words, would you categorize yourself as a "yesterday" person, a "today" person, or a "tomorrow" person? Why?

- What's your gut reaction to the word *tradition*? Positive? Negative? Neutral? Why?

- What are some traditional practices in your family, such as ways you celebrate Christmas or other special times? How meaningful are they to you?

- How would you describe your current church: traditional, traditionalist, or non-traditional? Explain why.

Option 2

Watch the opening dialogue and the famous song "Tradition" from the movie *Fiddler on the Roof*. Begin at about 0:02:00 (based on 0:00:00 at studio logo) with Tevye's explanation of the fiddler on the roof. Watch through to the end of the song at about 0:09:30.

After watching the clip (and singing along if you'd like!), discuss these questions:

- Why do Tevye and the other members of his village love tradition so much? Can you relate to their love of tradition? Why or why not?

- Modern society has broken away from many of the traditions of the past, such as those portrayed in the film. What are some social or cultural traditions from the past that you view as negative—traditions you're glad we are free of? What are some social or cultural traditions from the past that you view positively or that you wish were still a part of today's world?

- When it comes to the church, do you tend to view traditions from the past as a positive or negative thing? Why?

■ The Issue

- Whether or not you consider your church to be traditional, there are some patterns and practices your church values and regularly includes in a worship service. What are some things your congregation always does as a means of being faithful to Christ? What would be lost if we were to drop them?

In a *Christianity Today* article "The Future Lies in the Past," Chris Armstrong reflects on his early Christian experience saying,

> Yet through the years . . . I felt like we were missing something. . . . There was utterly no sense of the mystical massiveness of a church that had stood firmly for two thousand years. No sense that our foundation actually stretched down and back through time. I didn't have a clue who John Wesley, Martin Luther, Bernard of Clairvaux, and Ignatius of Antioch were. I just knew that I felt like I was part of a church that was in some ways powerful, but in other ways shallow and insecure in a threatening world that did not share our faith. I now see that my early sense of the church's insecurity stemmed from what J. I. Packer has called evangelicalism's "stunted ecclesiology," rooted in our alienation from our past.

- Can you relate to Armstrong? In your own evangelical experience, have you felt connected or disconnected from the church's past or from Christian history? Explain.

■ Reflect

Take a moment to read Mark 7:1–8; Colossians 2:6–10, 20–23; and 2 Peter 1:16–21 on your own. Record your observations: Which phrases or words jump out at you? What are the key ideas in these texts? How might these texts relate to tradition and the role it should (or should not) play in the church?

■ Let's Explore

Jesus both valued and critiqued traditions.
Read Matthew 5:17–20.

- What do you think Jesus meant when he said this? How would you explain this passage to a non-believer or to a new Christian?

Not only did Jesus embrace the commands and prophecies of Scripture, but Jesus also did not throw out the religious traditions in which he was reared. He went to the synagogue and the temple, he read and quoted from the Torah (our Old Testament), and he prayed the Psalms—all part of his culture's spiritual tradition. As a good Jew, he would have recited the *shema* twice daily: "Listen, people of Israel! The LORD our God is the only LORD. Love the LORD your God with all your heart, all your soul, and all your strength" (Deuteronomy 6:4–5). He accepted the Ten Commandments given to Moses as an expression of God's will for how people should live, especially those belonging to the covenant community.

- Why do you think it was important for Jesus to embrace many of the traditions of his culture and of Scripture? What value do you think he found in the worship traditions he took part in?

By the time Jesus came along, the Jewish religious establishment—the rabbis and what the Gospel writers refer to as the "scribes and Pharisees"—had developed rules for everything from personal hygiene to conduct on the Sabbath to almsgiving. The intention of these rules and regulations was good—to help people adhere to the will of God as they understood it and to keep people from being lured by the temptations of the world. But these rules and regulations gave people the sense that salvation could be earned by adherence to those rules.

Yet Jesus did not feel bound by these rules and regulations, which often got him into trouble with the Pharisees. Read one such example in Mark 7:1–8.

- How should Jesus's words in Mark 7:8 be applied? Do you think "human teachings" (also translated as "the traditions of men") have a place in the church? How would you make your case to someone who disagreed with you on this point?

We need to distinguish between faith-strengthening traditions and human traditions that undermine the gospel, the lordship of Jesus Christ, or the Christian life.

Tradition in the Greek New Testament can be both a noun and a verb. Sometimes it was used in the New Testament to refer to the gospel itself and the apostles' teaching about the life, death, and resurrection of Jesus. But it could also refer to a process—either the keeping of the faith or passing it on to others. Hence, three things are needed to maintain Christian faithfulness over time: 1) we must receive the faith, making it our own; 2) we need to keep the faith (that is, remain faithful to the truth of God's revelation); and 3) we must pass on the faith to others. All three movements are necessary for faith to remain a living reality, a life-giving tradition.

Read 2 Thessalonians 2:15 (if you have time, also read 1 Corinthians 11:2 and 2 Thessalonians 3:6.) Notice that in these verses the New Century Version (and other more modern translations such as the NIV) renders the Greek for *tradition* as *teaching*. Other more formal translations, such as

SESSION 3: TRADITION: LOVE IT OR LOSE IT?

the New King James and the New Revised Standard Version use the word *tradition*.

- What traditions (or teachings) do you think Paul wants his readers to stand strong in? Why do you think these traditions were so important to Paul and to the early church?

Read Colossians 2:6–10, 20–23.

- Here, rather than using "tradition" (or "teaching") positively, Paul warns against human worldviews and practices that oppose the gospel. How are we to distinguish between human traditions which are positive and faith-strengthening and human traditions that are dangerous, such as those Paul references or those referred to by Jesus in Mark 7:8?

In "The Future Lies in the Past," Armstrong highlights the cautions of Joel Scandrett, who warned evangelicals against these three common and mistaken approaches to tradition:

1. *Anachronism*: naively interpreting the tradition in light of contemporary assumptions;

2. *Traditionalism*: being unwilling to see the flaws in the early church's traditions;

3. *Eclecticism*: selectively appropriating ancient practices without regard to their original purposes or contexts.

- Which of these errors do you think is most common among evangelicals? Which do you think is most dangerous? Why?

In his article, Olsen explains what he views as the proper understanding of Christian tradition and its relationship with Scripture this way:

> An analogy is the United States Constitution and the history of landmark Supreme Court decisions that serve as precedents for later decisions. Judges and lawyers must know the precedents, but the Constitution is the supreme authority. Landmark decisions of earlier courts can be overturned if they are judged to be inconsistent with the Constitution. No competent judge, however, simply tosses out the history of court decisions. They serve as secondary authorities, guides to interpretation.
>
> So it is with the Bible and the Great Tradition. Evangelicals should study the tradition, for we are not the first to seek answers to difficult questions and problems in theology. However, we must not elevate the tradition to inviolable, authoritative status.

- In your opinion, what is the proper relationship between Scripture and Christian traditions? Do you find Olsen's analogy helpful? Why or why not? If not, where does it break down? If so, what makes it helpful?

As we grow toward spiritual maturity, we need the insights, correction, and examples of others—including the saints who have gone before us.

The "Chicago Call" of the 1970s was an important moment when the evangelical church began to look at the past as it marked a path toward the future. Part of that document read,

> We confess that we have often lost the fullness of our Christian heritage, too readily assuming that the Scripture and the Spirit make us independent of the past. In so doing, we have become theologically shallow, spiritually weak, blind to the work of God in others and married to our cultures.

- How has too marked an independence from the past made the evangelical church shallow or weak?

Read 2 Peter 1:16–21 and 3:14–18.

There will always be some people with unorthodox understanding of Scripture and doctrine. They will twist the truth of the revelation of God in Christ to fit idiosyncratic notions or to justify their sinful actions. Cults, for instance, take some truth about the faith and turn it inside out or make some minor doctrine the center of the faith. This was so from the beginning of the church.

Peter noted how the original giving of Scripture wasn't a matter of mere human inspiration. Rather, men and women, moved by the Holy Spirit, received and gave utterance to the Word of God that was revealed to them. In like matter, the interpretation of Scripture needs Holy Spirit guidance. And one way Holy Spirit guidance comes is through the testing of our insights and interpretations with other Christians in the body of faith. Another way is to learn from those Christians who have gone before us. There is a body of literature to help us discern the meaning of Scripture (commentaries, creeds and confessions of faith, theological treatises, liturgies for worship, ethical exhortations), and countless Christians have lived out the faith before us, leaving us models of faithfulness. That is part of our tradition, our heritage as Christians. We ignore it at our peril and loss.

- Through its history, the church has formulated creeds and confessions of faith. Do you think creeds or confessions of faith are essential means of keeping the church true to God's revelation? Or do they get in the way of faithfulness to Scripture or the application of Scripture to new contexts and challenges?

- On a personal level, have you had experiences or practices based on church history or tradition that have strengthened your faith? For example, have ancient prayers or traditional hymns spoken to you? Have the words of a creed steadied you? Have you been ministered to by your church tradition of communion? Share a specific example of something from the Christian tradition that has helped you grow in faith.

Hebrews 12:1 reminds us that "We are surrounded by a great cloud of people whose lives tell us what faith means." Believing is only one part of the Christian faith; behaving is another. We have the lives of the saints, including many who were martyred for their faith, as part of our tradition. These lives give us examples of Spirit-filled disciples of Jesus.

- Who are some Christians from the past (whether ancient past or recent past) whose lives or writings have inspired you? How have their words or life stories affected you?

■ Going Forward

Read the following together as a group then discuss the final questions:

There are two impulses in Protestantism. One comes from Philipp Melanchthon, Martin Luther's sidekick during the Protestant Reformation, whose motto was *non nova dogmata* (no new doctrines). "I have many times stated emphatically that I am neither an originator nor an advocate of new teachings," said Melanchthon, an ironic statement for one involved

SESSION 3: TRADITION: LOVE IT OR LOSE IT?

in one of the most innovative movements in church history. The other impulse comes from the Puritan preacher, John Robinson, who told the pilgrims before they set sail for the New World: "The Lord hath more truth and light yet to break forth out of his Holy Word," which became the inspiration for George Rawson's hymn text, "We limit not the truth of God." Of the Calvinists in his day, Robinson said, "They stick where [Calvin] left them, a misery much to be lamented." For Robinson, church tradition could not contain or circumscribe the Word of God, and to open ourselves to the new truth God has in store for us, we need to keep going back to his Word.

- Which viewpoint do you tend to lean more toward: Melanchthon or Robinson? What strengths does each perspective bring? What weaknesses?

- It is said that some churches need a good dose of solvent, other churches need glue. In the first instance, there is so much rigidity that something drastic is needed to get them unstuck. In the latter one, everything is always in flux and something is needed to give them solidity and coherence. Which do you think your church is in more need of—solvent or glue? Or some of both? Where in your church life would you apply the solvent? The glue?

Pray together, asking God to guide your church as you chart your future path. Conclude your time together with a traditional worship practice that's comfortable for your group, such as singing a much-loved hymn, reciting a creed, or praying the Lord's Prayer.

CURRENT ISSUES: THE FUTURE OF THE CHURCH

Is emerging Christianity the answer to postmodern challenges?

SCRIPTURE FOCUS

John 17:20–23

Acts 17:16–33

1 Corinthians 9:19–23

2 Timothy 2:1–2, 15

James 2:14–18

SESSION 4

THE EMERGING FUTURE CHURCH?

■

Since the mid-1990s, many writers and ministers have considered postmodernism to be the single greatest threat facing Christianity today. Skepticism, ambiguity, and paradox—among other characteristics of postmodern thought—potentially undermine Christian belief, which is based on faith in a true and unchanging God. How do we live out and explain the gospel among a doubtful generation? In recent years the emerging church movement has developed in part to respond to that very question. Some herald the emerging church movement as a healthy re-thinking of church dogma and entrenched culture. Others critique the movement for loose theology and for a perceived arrogance toward "regular" churches. We'll discuss whether the emerging movement is a positive or negative trend for the church's future.

Before You Meet

Read "Five Streams of the Emerging Church" by Scot McKnight from *Christianity Today*.

FIVE STREAMS OF THE EMERGING CHURCH

Key elements of the most controversial and misunderstood movement in the church today.

by Scot McKnight

It is said that emerging Christians confess their faith like mainliners—meaning they say things publicly they don't really believe. They drink like Southern Baptists—meaning, to adapt some words from Mark Twain, they are teetotalers when it is judicious. They talk like Catholics—meaning they cuss and use naughty words. They evangelize and theologize like the Reformed—meaning they rarely evangelize, yet theologize all the time. They worship like charismatics—meaning with their whole bodies, some parts tattooed. They vote like Episcopalians—meaning they eat, drink, and sleep on their left side. And, they deny the truth—meaning they've got a latte-soaked copy of Derrida in their smoke- and beer-stained backpacks.

Along with unfair stereotypes of other traditions, such are the urban legends surrounding the emerging church—one of the most controversial and misunderstood movements today. As a theologian, I have studied the movement and interacted with its key leaders for years—even more, I happily consider myself part of this movement or "conversation." As an evangelical, I've had my concerns, but overall I think what emerging Christians bring to the table is vital for the overall health of the church.

In this article, I want to undermine the urban legends and provide a more accurate description of the emerging movement. Though the movement has an international dimension, I will focus on the North American scene.

SESSION 4: THE EMERGING FUTURE CHURCH?

To define a movement, we must, as a courtesy, let it say what it is. Eddie Gibbs and Ryan Bolger, in their book, *Emerging Churches: Creating Christian Community in Postmodern Cultures* (Baker Academic, 2005) define "emerging" in this way:

> Emerging churches are communities that practice the way of Jesus within postmodern cultures. This definition encompasses nine practices. Emerging churches (1) identify with the life of Jesus, (2) transform the secular realm, and (3) live highly communal lives. Because of these three activities, they (4) welcome the stranger, (5) serve with generosity, (6) participate as producers, (7) create as created beings, (8) lead as a body, and (9) take part in spiritual activities.

This definition is both descriptive and analytical. D. A. Carson's *Becoming Conversant with the Emerging Church* (Zondervan, 2005) is not alone in pointing to the problems in the emerging movement, and I shall point out a few myself in what follows. But as a description of the movement, Carson's book lacks firsthand awareness and suffers from an overly narrow focus—on Brian McLaren and postmodern epistemology.

To prevent confusion, a distinction needs to be made between "emerging" and "Emergent." Emerging is the wider, informal, global, ecclesial (church-centered) focus of the movement, while Emergent is an official organization in the U.S. and the U.K. Emergent Village, the organization, is directed by Tony Jones, a Ph.D. student at Princeton Theological Seminary and a world traveler on behalf of all things both Emergent and emerging. Other names connected with Emergent Village include Doug Pagitt, Chris Seay, Tim Keel, Karen Ward, Ivy Beckwith, Brian McLaren, and Mark Oestreicher. Emergent U.K. is directed by Jason Clark. While Emergent is the intellectual and philosophical network of the emerging movement, it is a mistake to narrow all of emerging to the Emergent Village.

"Emerging" catches into one term the global reshaping of how to "do church" in postmodern culture. It has no central offices, and it is as varied as evangelicalism itself. If I were to point to one centrist expression of the emerging movement in the U.S., it would be Dan Kimball's Vintage Church in Santa Cruz, California. His U.K. counterpart is Andrew Jones, known on the internet as Tall Skinny Kiwi. Jones is a world-traveling speaker, teacher, and activist for simple churches, house churches, and churches without worship services.

Following are five themes that characterize the emerging movement. I see them as streams flowing into the emerging lake. No one says the emerging movement is the only group of Christians doing these things, but together they crystallize into the emerging movement.

Prophetic (or At Least Provocative)

One of the streams flowing into the emerging lake is prophetic rhetoric. The emerging movement is consciously and deliberately provocative. Emerging Christians believe the church needs to change, and they are beginning to live as if that change had already occurred. Since I swim in the emerging lake, I can self-critically admit that we sometimes exaggerate.

Our language frequently borrows the kind of rhetoric found in Old Testament prophets like Hosea: "For I desire mercy, not sacrifice, and acknowledgment of God rather than burnt offerings" (6:6). Hosea engages here in deliberate overstatement, for God never forbids Temple worship. In a similar way, none in the emerging crowd is more rhetorically effective than Brian McLaren in *Generous Orthodoxy*: "Often I don't think Jesus would be caught dead as a Christian, were he physically here today. . . . Generally, I don't think Christians would like Jesus if he showed up today as he did two thousand years ago. In fact, I think we'd call him a heretic and plot to kill him too." McLaren, on the very next page, calls this statement an exaggeration. Still, the rhetoric is in place.

Consider this quote from an Irish emerging Christian, Peter Rollins, author of *How (Not) to Speak of God* (Paraclete, 2006): "Thus orthodoxy is no longer (mis)understood as the opposite of heresy but rather is understood as a term that signals a way of being in the world rather than a means of believing things about the world." The age-old canard of orthodoxy versus orthopraxy plays itself out once again.

Such rhetoric makes its point, but it sometimes divides. I hope those of us who use it (and this critique can't be restricted to the emerging movement) will learn when to avoid such language.

Postmodern

Mark Twain said the mistake God made was in not forbidding Adam to eat the serpent. Had God forbidden the serpent, Adam would certainly have eaten him. When the evangelical world prohibited postmodernity, as if it were fruit from the forbidden tree, the postmodern "fallen" among us—like F. LeRon Shults, Jamie Smith, Kevin Vanhoozer, John Franke, and Peter Rollins—chose to eat it to see what it might taste like. We found that it tasted good, even if at times we found ourselves spitting out hard chunks of nonsense. A second stream of emerging water is postmodernism.

Postmodernity cannot be reduced to the denial of truth. Instead, it is the collapse of inherited metanarratives (overarching explanations of life) like those of science or Marxism. Why have they collapsed? Because of the impossibility of getting outside their assumptions.

While there are good as well as naughty consequences of opting for a postmodern stance (and not all in the emerging movement are as careful as they should be), evangelical Christians can rightfully embrace certain elements of postmodernity. Jamie Smith, a professor at Calvin College, argues in *Who's Afraid of Postmodernity?* (Baker Academic, 2006) that such thinking is compatible, in some ways, with classical Augustinian epistemology. No one points the way forward in this regard more carefully than longtime missionary to India Lesslie Newbigin, especially in his book *Proper Confidence: Faith, Doubt, and Certainty in Christian Discipleship* (Eerdmans, 1995). Emerging upholds faith seeking understanding, and trust preceding the apprehension or comprehension of gospel truths.

Living as a Christian in a postmodern context means different things to different people. Some—to borrow categories I first heard from Doug Pagitt, pastor at Solomon's Porch in Minneapolis—will minister *to* postmoderns, others *with* postmoderns, and still others *as* postmoderns.

David Wells at Gordon-Conwell Theological Seminary falls into the *to* category, seeing postmoderns as trapped in moral relativism and epistemological bankruptcy out of which they must be rescued.

Others minister *with* postmoderns. That is, they live with, work with, and converse with postmoderns, accepting their postmodernity as a fact of life in our world. Such Christians view postmodernity as a present condition into which we are called to proclaim and live out the gospel.

The vast majority of emerging Christians and churches fit these first two categories. They don't deny truth, they don't deny that Jesus Christ is truth, and they don't deny the Bible is truth.

The third kind of emerging postmodernity attracts all the attention. Some have chosen to minister *as* postmoderns. That is, they embrace the idea that we cannot know absolute truth, or, at least, that we cannot know truth absolutely. They speak of the end of metanarratives and the importance of social location in shaping one's view of truth. They frequently express nervousness about propositional truth. LeRon Shults, formerly a professor of theology at Bethel Theological Seminary, writes:

> From a theological perspective, this fixation with propositions can easily lead to the attempt to use the finite tool of language on an absolute Presence that transcends and embraces all finite reality. Languages are culturally constructed symbol systems that enable humans to communicate by designating one finite reality in distinction from another. The truly infinite God of Christian faith is beyond all our linguistic grasping, as all the great theologians from Irenaeus to Calvin have insisted, and so the struggle to capture God in our finite propositional structures is nothing short of linguistic idolatry.

Praxis-oriented

The emerging movement's connection to postmodernity may grab attention and garner criticism, but what most characterizes emerging is the stream best called *praxis*—how the faith is lived out. At its core, the emerging movement is an attempt to fashion a new ecclesiology (doctrine of the church). Its distinctive emphases can be seen in its worship, its concern with orthopraxy, and its missional orientation.

Worship: I've heard folks describe the emerging movement as "funky worship" or "candles and incense" or "smells and bells." It's true; many in the emerging movement are creative, experiential, and sensory in their worship gatherings.

Evangelicals sometimes forget that God cares about sacred space and ritual—he told Moses how to design the tabernacle and gave detailed directions to Solomon for building a majestic Temple. Neither Jesus nor

Paul said much about aesthetics, but the author of Hebrews did. And we should not forget that some Reformers, knowing the power of aesthetics, stripped churches clean of all artwork.

Some emerging Christians see churches with pulpits in the center of a hall-like room with hard, wooden pews lined up in neat rows, and they wonder if there is another way to express—theologically, aesthetically, and anthropologically—what we do when we gather. They ask these sorts of questions: Is the sermon the most important thing on Sunday morning? If we sat in a circle would we foster a different theology and praxis? If we lit incense, would we practice our prayers differently? If we put the preacher on the same level as the congregation, would we create a clearer sense of the priesthood of all believers? If we acted out what we believe, would we encounter more emphatically the Incarnation?

Orthopraxy: A notable emphasis of the emerging movement is orthopraxy, that is, right living. The contention is that *how a person lives* is more important than *what he or she believes*. Many will immediately claim that we need both or that orthopraxy flows from orthodoxy. Most in the emerging movement agree we need both, but they contest the second claim: experience does not prove that those who *believe* the right things *live* the right way. No matter how much sense the traditional connection makes, it does not necessarily work itself out in practice. Public scandals in the church—along with those not made public—prove this point time and again.

Here is an emerging, provocative way of saying it: "By their fruits [not their theology] you will know them." As Jesus's brother James said, "Faith without works is dead." Rhetorical exaggerations aside, I know of no one in the emerging movement who believes that one's relationship with God is established by how one lives. Nor do I know anyone who thinks that it doesn't matter what one believes about Jesus Christ. But the focus is shifted. Gibbs and Bolger define emerging churches as those who practice "the way of Jesus" in the postmodern era.

Jesus declared that we will be judged according to how we treat the least of these (Matt. 25:31–46) and that the wise man is the one who *practices* the words of Jesus (Matt. 7:24–27). In addition, every judgment scene in the Bible is portrayed as a judgment based on works; no judgment scene looks like a theological articulation test.

Missional: The foremost concern of the praxis stream is being *missional*. What does this mean? First, the emerging movement becomes missional by participating, with God, in the redemptive work of God in this world. In essence, it joins with the apostle Paul in saying that God has given us "the ministry of reconciliation" (2 Cor. 5:18).

Second, it seeks to become missional by participating in the community where God's redemptive work occurs. The church is the community through which God works and in which God manifests the credibility of the gospel.

Third, becoming missional means participating in the holistic redemptive work of God in this world. The Spirit groans, the creation groans, and we groan for the redemption of God (see Rom. 8:18–27).

This holistic emphasis finds perfect expression in the ministry of Jesus, who went about doing good to bodies, spirits, families, and societies. He picked the marginalized up from the floor and put them back in their seats at the table; he attracted harlots and tax collectors; he made the lame walk and opened the ears of the deaf. He cared, in other words, not just about lost souls, but also about whole persons and whole societies.

Post-evangelical

A fourth stream flowing into the emerging lake is characterized by the term *post-evangelical*. The emerging movement is a protest against much of evangelicalism as currently practiced. It is post-evangelical in the way that neo-evangelicalism (in the 1950s) was post-fundamentalist. It would not be unfair to call it postmodern evangelicalism. This stream flows from the conviction that the church must always be reforming itself.

The vast majority of emerging Christians are evangelical theologically. But they are post-evangelical in at least two ways.

Post-systematic theology: The emerging movement tends to be suspicious of systematic theology. Why? Not because we don't read systematics, but because the diversity of theologies alarms us, no genuine consensus has been achieved, God didn't reveal a systematic theology but a storied narrative, and no language is capable of capturing the Absolute Truth who alone is God. Frankly, the emerging movement loves ideas and theology. It just doesn't have an airtight system or statement of faith. We believe the Great Tradition offers various ways for telling the truth about God's redemption in Christ, but we don't believe any one theology gets it absolutely right.

Hence, a trademark feature of the emerging movement is that we believe all theology will remain a conversation about the Truth, who is God in Christ through the Spirit; and about God's story of redemption at work in the church. No systematic theology can be final. In this sense, the emerging movement is radically Reformed. It turns its chastened epistemology against itself, saying, "This is what I believe, but I could be wrong. What do you think? Let's talk."

In versus out: An admittedly controversial element of post-evangelicalism is that many in the emerging movement are skeptical about the "in versus out" mentality of much of evangelicalism. Even if one is an exclusivist (believing that there is a dividing line between Christians and non-Christians), the issue of who is in and who is out pains the emerging generation.

Some emerging Christians point to the words of Jesus: "Whoever is not against us is for us" (Mark 9:40). Others, borrowing the words of the old hymn, point to a "wideness in God's mercy." Still others take postmodernity's crushing of metanarratives and extend that to master theological narratives—like Christianity. They say what really matters is orthopraxy and that it doesn't matter which religion one belongs to, as long as one loves God and one's neighbor as one's self. Some even accept Spencer Burke's unbiblical contention in *A Heretic's Guide to Eternity* (Jossey-Bass, 2006) that all are born "in" and only some "opt out."

This emerging ambivalence about who is in and who is out creates a serious problem for evangelism. The emerging movement is not known for it, but I wish it were. Unless you proclaim the Good News of Jesus Christ, there is no good news at all—and if there is no Good News, then there is no Christianity, emerging or evangelical.

Personally, I'm an evangelist. Not so much the tract-toting, door-knocking kind, but the Jesus-talking and Jesus-teaching kind. I spend time praying in my office before class and pondering about how to teach in order to bring home the message of the gospel.

So I offer here a warning to the emerging movement: any movement that is not evangelistic is failing the Lord. We may be humble about what we believe, and we may be careful to make the gospel and its commitments clear, but we must always keep the proper goal in mind: summoning everyone to follow Jesus Christ and to discover the redemptive work of God in Christ through the Spirit of God.

Political

A final stream flowing into the emerging lake is politics. Tony Jones is regularly told that the emerging movement is a latte-drinking, backpack-lugging, Birkenstock-wearing group of twenty-first-century, left-wing, hippie wannabes. Put directly, they are Democrats. And that spells "post" for conservative-evangelical-politics-as-usual.

I have publicly aligned myself with the emerging movement. What attracts me is its soft postmodernism (or critical realism) and its praxis/missional focus. I also lean left in politics. I tell my friends that I have voted Democrat for years for all the wrong reasons. I don't think the Democratic Party is worth a hoot, but its historic commitment to the poor and to centralizing government for social justice is what I think government should do. I don't support abortion—in fact, I think it is immoral. I believe in civil rights, but I don't believe homosexuality is God's design. And, like many in the emerging movement, I think the Religious Right doesn't see what it is doing. Books like Randy Balmer's *Thy Kingdom Come: An Evangelical's Lament: How the Religious Right Distorts the Faith and Threatens America* (Basic Books, 2006) and David Kuo's *Tempting Faith: An Inside Story of Political Seduction* (Free Press, 2006) make their rounds in emerging circles because they say things we think need to be said.

Sometimes, however, when I look at emerging politics, I see Walter Rauschenbusch, the architect of the social gospel. Without trying to deny the spiritual gospel, he led his followers into the social gospel. The results were devastating for mainline Christianity's ability to summon sinners to personal conversion. The results were also devastating for evangelical Christianity, which has itself struggled to maintain a proper balance.

I ask my fellow emerging Christians to maintain their missional and ecclesial focus, just as I urge my fellow evangelicals to engage in the social as well.

All in all, it is unlikely that the emerging movement will disappear anytime soon. If I were a prophet, I'd say that it will influence most of evangelicalism in its chastened epistemology (if it hasn't already), its emphasis on praxis, and its missional orientation. I see the emerging movement much like the Jesus and charismatic movements of the 1960s, which undoubtedly have found a place in the quilt called evangelicalism.

Scot McKnight is professor of religious studies at North Park Theological Seminary in Chicago, Illinois. He is author of The Jesus Creed *(Paraclete, 2004) and, most recently,* The Real Mary: Why Evangelicals Can Embrace the Mother of Jesus *(Paraclete, 2006). This article is condensed and adapted from a lecture given at Westminster Theological Seminary, Philadelphia, in October 2006. See the blog JesusCreed.org for more of McKnight's emerging musings. "Five Streams of the Emerging Church" was first published in* Christianity Today, *February 2007.*

■ Open Up

Choose one of the following activities to launch your discussion time.

Option 1

Discuss these icebreaker questions:

- Can you remember a time when you began to think your parents had completely lost touch with the culture? Give an example.

- If you're a parent, also give an example of something you do or wear or listen to that convinces your children that you are behind the times.

Option 2

Each group member should grab a sheet of paper and a pen. First write down three to five words or phrases that your parents use (or used) and that you consider old-fashioned. Next, write down three to five words or phrases your child or someone from a younger generation uses that you consider absurd or silly.

Now divide into two or three smaller groups. Exchange all your papers with those of another group; read aloud all the words written on your new papers. Discuss:

- Why do you think different generations use different terms and phrases? What influences our language?

- Do you relate better to the generation that's older than you or the generation that's younger than you? Why?

■ The Issue

- In what ways do you think your home church has lost touch with culture? Or in what ways has your church sought to be culturally relevant?

In "Five Streams of the Emerging Church," Scot McKnight celebrates the fact that the emerging movement will eventually influence "most of evangelicalism in its chastened epistemology, its emphasis on praxis, and its missional orientation." Others are more hesitant and suggest that the movement is fractured and appeals to only a slice of the younger population.

- What experience, if any, have you had with the emerging church movement? If you've attended an emerging church, share what it was like. If you haven't been to an emerging church, would you like to visit one? Why or why not?

- Based on what you've read in these articles as well as what you've heard or experienced, are you encouraged by the emerging movement or suspicious of it? Why?

■ Reflect

Take a moment to read John 17:20–23, Acts 17:16–33, 1 Corinthians 9:19–23, 2 Timothy 2:1–2, 15; and James 2:14–18 on your own. Jot down a few notes and observations about the passages. What do you find surprising or interesting about these passages? How do they relate to the articles you read for today's study?

■ Let's Explore

The church should minister within our postmodern culture.

Andy Crouch has described postmodernism as a way of thinking in which "modern values like objectivity, analysis, and control will become less compelling" and will be "superseded by postmodern values like mystery and wonder."

- What are some of the challenges of communicating the gospel in a culture that prefers mystery over certainty? How have you encountered these challenges personally?

When Paul shared the gospel in Athens in Acts 17:16–33, his presentation was different than when he preached to the Jews (see Acts 13:14–43 for comparison). This was in part because he knew that Athenians and Jews understood the world in radically different ways.

- What similarities, if any, do you see between Paul's ministry to the Athenians and emerging church ministry among postmoderns? What are some differences?

Paul says in 1 Corinthians 9:19–23 that he was called to become "all things to all people" in order to win as many people to Christ as possible.

- Do you think everyone (including you) is called to communicate the gospel in a postmodern context? Why or why not? If so, what might it mean for the church to "become" postmodern in order to reach postmoderns?

The church should uphold both sound doctrine and Christ-like living.

Rob Bell, high-profile pastor of Mars Hill church, says that he and his wife are "rediscovering Christianity as . . . a way of life. We grew up in churches where people knew the nine verses [that explain] why we don't speak in tongues, but had never experienced the overwhelming presence of God."

- What do you think Bell means when he says that Christianity is "a way of life"?

- How does this compare or contrast with your own experience in the church? Does your home church tend to put greater emphasis on understanding doctrine or living out one's faith?

SESSION 4: THE EMERGING FUTURE CHURCH?

According to Scot McKnight, this emphasis on putting faith into action is a distinctive trait of the emerging church; it may take the form of intimate, experiential worship, social service, or political activity.

Re-read James 2:14–18.

- In what ways does the emerging church fulfill James's requirements for authentic Christian faith? In what ways does your home church live out this passage?

In 2 Timothy 2:1–2 and 15, Paul encourages his younger colleague Timothy to be careful to teach right doctrine and to train other people how to teach right doctrine.

- How do you think this passage applies in today's increasingly postmodern context? What place can postmodern values like questioning, mystery, tolerance, and open-mindedness have in Christian faith? Or do they have a place at all?

- From what you've read and from your experience with emerging churches, do you think they fulfill Paul's charge to be people who correctly handle the word of truth? Share examples.

- In your opinion, is there any real distinction between believing the right things and living the right way? Why or why not? If so, which do you spend more energy developing—doctrinal correctness or appropriate behavior?

The church should strive for unity.
Kristin Bell recalls her own sense of dissatisfaction with her church, saying, "Life in the church had become so small . . . It had worked for me for a long time. Then it stopped working." Like Kristin, many in the emerging church movement are disaffected evangelicals whose frustrations have led them to leave their old church in order to start or join something new.

- In what ways are some of the emerging church's criticisms of the modern church—particularly its inability to relate or reach out to postmodern culture—accurate? Or in what ways are their critiques off-base?

A quick search on the internet will reveal an immediate glimpse of the volatile schism that exists between some emerging church leaders and traditional evangelical leaders. One side accuses the other of heresy, worldliness, and arrogance; the other volleys back with accusations of being pharisaical, dead, and irrelevant.

- Read John 17:20–23. Jesus highly valued unity in the church. So is the emerging church movement just one more example of splintering and disunity? Or is it a valid evidence of growth and positive change?

- Do you think it's possible to critique problems in the church without being divisive? Explain.

■ Going Forward

Read the following quotation as a group:

The church today is at a critical juncture in regard to two major societal changes. The first . . . is the generational transition from the Baby Boom generation to Generation X and the Millennial generation . . . The second change is a cultural shift . . . from the Enlightenment/modern era to the emerging/postmodern era. How the church responds to these generational changes and—even more importantly—to these cultural changes will determine how faithful and successful the church will be in the twenty-first century in accomplishing God's mission for the church.
—Jimmy Long in *Emerging Hope*

- What lessons can you—individually and as a group—learn from the emerging church about ministering in a postmodern culture?

- Which of the movement's limitations do you hope to avoid?

Divide into pairs for a brief prayer. Pray that your partner will develop relationships with people both younger and older than him or her. Pray that they may better understand the cultural changes underway and how best to respond.

Is it possible to overcome our racial barriers and be the unified church God has called us to be?

SCRIPTURE FOCUS

Isaiah 56:3–8

Acts 2:42–47, 4:32–33

Galatians 3:26–28

SESSION 5

MULTIRACIAL CONGREGATIONS

■

Have you ever wondered what God thinks about the church being the most segregated of all communities? In this study we will take a look at the cultural history and diversity of the New Testament church as we seek to integrate all peoples and nations into the church of Jesus Christ. How would true integration affect the life of the church as a whole if we dared to take the challenge? Are we truly prepared for what would come next? These are some of the questions we will discuss in this Bible study, as we read how four pastors from the Latino, Asian, black, and white communities respond in *United by Faith,* a book that calls for pursuing multiracial churches as the biblical pattern.

■ Before You Meet

Read "Harder Than Anyone Can Imagine" from *Christianity Today*.

HARDER THAN ANYONE CAN IMAGINE

Four working pastors—Latino, Asian, black, and white—respond to the thesis of United by Faith: The Multiracial Congregation as an Answer to the Problem of Race *by Curtiss Paul DeYoung, Michael O. Emerson, George Yancey, and Karen Chai Kim (Oxford University Press).*

This round-table discussion of *United by Faith* included pastors Noel Castellanos, Bill Hybels, Soong-Chan Rah, and Frank Reid; it was moderated by CT editor-at-large Edward Gilbreath and managing editor Mark Galli. Noel Castellanos is the founder and president of the Latino Leadership Foundation, and was founding pastor of La Villita Community Church in inner-city Chicago. Bill Hybels is senior pastor of Willow Creek Community Church in South Barrington, Illinois, one of the most influential congregations in the United States. Soong-Chan Rah is senior pastor of Cambridge Community Fellowship Church, a multiethnic, urban-ministry-focused church reaching postmoderns in Cambridge, Massachusetts. Frank Reid is senior pastor of the historic Bethel African Methodist Episcopal Church in Baltimore.

The main argument of *United by Faith* is that Christian churches, "when possible," should be multiracial. What is your gut-level reaction to that assertion?

Reid: I think it is valid and necessary. The challenge is similar to the moment in Galatians 2 when Peter and Paul clash on fellowshipping with Gentiles. What the early Christians did not have to deal with to the same extent that we do today is how race has become an idol. On both sides of the racial divide, so much is twisted by the social constructs we've formed and cling to about race.

Castellanos: God has made clear that in Christ we're all one. There is no Greek, no Jew, no Gentile, no male or female. But from my

SESSION 5: MULTIRACIAL CONGREGATIONS

experiences, both inside and outside the church, multicultural fellowship is a lot harder to achieve than anybody can ever imagine.

When I first went into full-time ministry in a majority white organization, I naïvely embraced the theology that in Christ we're one—and that even though we were in a Mexican community, we could be one with our Caucasian brothers and sisters and anybody else. But as you try to live that out, you realize there are incredible implications. It's not easy.

Rah: If the statistics in the book bear out, it means that less than 6 percent of American churches are multiethnic, given what I think are the authors' fairly generous guidelines of 80 percent of one ethnic group and 20 percent of another. Those are pretty wide guidelines, and still less than 6 percent of American churches approach that.

If we were to hear of any other institution in the United States that had those kinds of statistics, we would be outraged. If less than 6 percent of universities or government institutions were integrated, we would say there is something seriously wrong.

Hybels: Willow Creek started in the era when, as the book noted, the church-growth people were saying, "Don't dissipate any of your energies fighting race issues. Focus everything on evangelism." It was the homogeneous unit principle of church growth. And I remember as a young pastor thinking, *That's true.* I didn't know whether I wanted to chance alienating people who were seekers, whose eternity was on the line, and who might only come to church one time. I wanted to take away as many obstacles as possible, other than the Cross, to help people focus on the gospel.

So now, thirty years later, as I read this book, I recognize that a true biblically functioning community must include being multiethnic. My heart beats so fast for that vision today. I marvel at how naive and pragmatic I was thirty years ago.

What were your "aha" moments on this issue?

Hybels: Alvin Bibbs is an African American who leads our extension ministry and helps us with our inner-city partnerships. A few years back, when I was leaving to go on a family vacation, I said to Alvin as I was walking out the door, "God's stirring in me about the reconciliation issue. If you can give me one book on the issue to take with me, I'll read it while I'm gone." He grabbed the book *Divided by Faith,* and I took it with me on that weeklong vacation. And that book just wrecked me.

I was like the stereotypical person that *Divided by Faith* talked about. I didn't view myself as being racist in any way. I therefore felt that there was no issue I was responsible for. If it was okay with me and my individual multiracial friendships, then it was all okay. And when I got to the section about the ongoing structural inequities, it devastated me. I thought, *How could I have not seen this?* And that was the beginning of my journey. I felt so badly about being a pastor for twenty-five years and having been as oblivious as I was to these kinds of issues. It was embarrassing. But these days I'm trying to make up for lost time.

Reid: One moment came in 1990 when Taylor Branch, a white author of two acclaimed books on Dr. Martin Luther King Jr., spoke to our congregation. We developed a friendship. And he said to me after about the third month of visiting, "Frank, I love the preaching. I love the work of the church. But you're so Afro-centric that, while my wife and I would love to join the church, I'm afraid our children will get nothing of their cultural heritage here." My internal response was, *Well, all these years black people in America have had to accept the white Jesus and white angels and a Euro-centric view of Christianity, so that's your problem.*

Shortly after that, though, we had a black member who is interracially married, but I didn't know it. So, in one of my sermons I regrettably made a negative reference to interracial marriages, and shortly thereafter she left the church. I saw her in a supermarket sometime later and asked her, as any pastor would, "Where are you now? How are you doing? Why did you leave?"

She said, "Pastor, you offended me because you were insensitive to people like my husband." Those two events led me to meet with Curtiss Paul DeYoung, one of the coauthors of this book, to talk about reconciliation and how to start a movement for multiracial Christianity.

While the authors recognize different types of multicultural churches, they hold up "integration" as the ideal. What does true integration look like to you?

Rah: One image that most of us have discarded by now is the "melting pot," because what it ends up becoming is a soupy mixture that has no flavor at all. A second metaphor is the "salad bowl," where you have all these different vegetables that sort of make up different flavors. But it turned out that the dressing was still creamy ranch, and it smothered everything else.

So we've got to start looking for other models that point to what we hope to become in a multicultural ministry. Are we looking to boil everybody down into one unrecognizable mass? Or are we trying to smother everything with one culture so that everybody is the same flavor? We need to be honest about this.

An African American at our church should get the sense that who he is as an African American believer is to be affirmed rather than subjugated. He shouldn't feel like he needs to become Asian or white to fit in. And that's one reason why this is so challenging, because it means we, as pastors, have to become cultural anthropologists in addition to all the other roles we fill.

Reid: This is where our theology becomes important, both in word and practice. If we're serious about building multicultural congregations, I think the church itself will become our new culture.

Castellanos: *United by Faith* draws on the thinking of Latino theologian Virgilio Elizondo, who talks about the *mestizaje* process of cultural mixing that took place in what's now the country of Mexico. The Spaniards blended with the dominant pre-Hispanic indigenous culture, and out of that was birthed the Mexican people. There were two contributing cultures, but it was a third culture that emerged.

The vision for multiethnic churches is not that people should leave behind their unique cultures, but that we should be able to come together to celebrate our diversity and to allow the blending of our differences to give birth to something new. I think there's an incredible amount of blessing in that.

Hybels: In the Willow Creek Association, we train pastors around the world. And probably the most intense experience I've ever had in this area of multiethnic ministry was in 2003 in South Africa, where after ten years of meeting with the various groups separately, we were finally able to bring together the whites and the coloreds and the blacks for a single conference. We trained a thousand people in the middle of Soweto, and when we sang a couple of songs together in that environment there wasn't a dry eye in the place. We spent the whole day talking about the power of community and what we could become if the church is working right.

So all this is about the challenge of keeping the value of culture, and having the power of Christian community be the galvanizing force that draws different people together.

How does that look at a big suburban church like Willow Creek?
Hybels: It would be very rare for you to come to Willow now and not see cultural diversity intentionally represented on our stage. You didn't see much for twenty-five years, but now we're very intentional about it, whether it's in our drama, in our worship team, in our band, or whoever is the host of the services, there's almost always going to be color and ethnicity represented. Again, we're still just in the embryonic stages, but our early attempts have been to celebrate the different cultures and to bet the farm that the power of Christ can bring us into something that's truly transcultural.

In every congregation, someone has to have a vision for what the church should be biblically and then the practicality to ask, *How do we move toward that?* In my opinion, a church doesn't have much of a chance of moving in the direction this book describes until the senior pastor has a "conversion experience" about this issue.

What in your experience has been the biggest obstacle to making multiracial churches work?
Reid: It's hard to talk about multiracial congregations without addressing the reality of spiritual warfare. Ephesians 6 says our struggle is not with flesh and blood but with the principalities and powers of evil.

SESSION 5: MULTIRACIAL CONGREGATIONS

Satan does not want to see unity in the church. And one way spiritual warfare manifests itself in everyday life is through the issue of power.

If a denomination or local church is going to become a true multiracial entity, that needs to be reflected in the composition of the leadership. But when you start talking about sharing power, that's usually when people get nervous.

Rah: Despite all the strides we've made with civil rights and racial reconciliation, American evangelicalism still looks dominated by white culture and white leadership.

One of the scriptures that we challenge our congregation with is Micah 4, which presents a picture of everybody laying down their swords in order to come to the house of God in humility. I think that image foreshadows people laying down their power to come into God's presence together.

Laying down power will mean different things for different communities, but I think for Asians the laying down of power means our willingness to make friendships across racial lines. We in the Asian community tend to be tight-knit within our own cultural circles, often to the exclusion of others. And I think with whites, laying down power comes down to a willingness to be in places of submission to those outside of their own community. How many whites have had non-white mentors?

Hybels: I think the way a Caucasian hears the power question is a little different. It has been a turnoff to me, because the language doesn't line up with our core values at Willow. Besides redemption itself, our church's highest value is servanthood.

It's never been about power. We've never recruited "powerful" people. We've watched God raise up people who have powerful and anointed ministries because they were humble and willing servants.

And so, that's an issue that pushes my buttons. But that's another reason why it's so helpful for me to be around tables like this one, because it helps me understand that the question is not so much about power-grabbing as it is about justice and inclusion.

But somehow, on all sides of this question, we have to do a better job with language, because in corporate America if someone talks about power, we all know what they mean. In church, however, power can stir up other notions.

As pastors, what have you done to encourage your congregations to be more multicultural?

Hybels: First, I had to communicate at a rate that could take people along with me as opposed to blowing the church up. If I'd done a month-long series after I read *Divided by Faith,* it would not have been constructive. I started by giving brief personal remarks about the issue, and that led eventually to sermons.

I also started working behind the scenes to give more visibility at our services to the various ethnic groups in our church. I wanted it to become a normal part of our church before having to declare some big change that people could fight against.

We also added an African American to our board and have been intentional in seeking out people of ethnicity when filling vacancies in our senior staff. We now offer classes on bridging the racial divide. And we're also doing Casa de Luz, which is a Spanish-speaking service in our chapel. Our feeling is we want to be a laboratory where we can practice this stuff, because I don't know how you learn unless you just dive in the pool and start swimming around.

What about smaller churches located in predominantly white, middle-class communities? How do they begin to bring more diversity to their churches?

Rah: I would imagine that most of CT's readers live in 99.9 percent white communities and have to travel to meet black folks and Asian folks and Hispanic folks. They would probably say, "It's not realistic for my church." But when you think of this in prophetic terms, as a biblical mandate, it brings more urgency.

The fact is, it's extremely difficult. In the past eight years since launching our church, we've seen numerous conflicts. There are moments when I say to myself, *It would be so much easier to go to a Korean church and pastor second-generation Koreans.* But it really comes back to the fact that this is God's calling. And I think churches

SESSION 5: MULTIRACIAL CONGREGATIONS

have to be secure in that. If it is not your calling, then you're going to burn out very quickly.

Reid: I'm still trying to discover the principles for making it work. I'm trying to figure out principles that I can take back to Bethel, sit down with our leaders and say, "This is what God is calling us to." And I know it's going to be hell, because the other side of having Asians and Hispanics and whites and African Americans and various ethnic groups worshiping together is sharing power in leadership. As long as you're sitting in the pew, it's fine. But as soon as you begin to grow and seek to use your gifts in positions of leadership and power, that's when the real challenge of the multiracial congregation begins.

Is such a vision so hard that we're never going to see anything but mere glimpses of true multiculturalism?

Hybels: I like C. S. Lewis's thinking in *Mere Christianity*. You have to weigh the progress of our sanctification against how miserable and cantankerous, funky and depraved people were before they met Christ. I believe what the authors have finally crystallized is something that the average pastor can wrap his or her brain around, and I think it's way too early to declare victory or defeat on this.

Castellanos: We can talk about this and write books about it until we're blue in the face, but ultimately the churches have to accept the challenge. We must create a movement of multiracial churches that is so compelling that people are going to say, "We cannot ignore this." The challenge for the church is this: Do you teach people the principles, or do you teach them to long for the reality of what God wants to see happen? Talking about it all the time can make the process methodical and taxing and burdensome. But when people are able to discover the biblical truth of multiracial churches for themselves, it becomes this contagious and liberating passion.

Rah: My three-year-old daughter is just at that age where she's starting to recognize different ethnicities, and I'm so excited because she now thinks it's normal to have a Haitian auntie, a Jamaican uncle, a Caucasian big sister, to have half of her friends be biracial. That is the kind of environment that I want for my kids, and this is a part of what the church is all about. That vision keeps me going.

Edward Gilbreath is director of editorial for Urban Ministries, Inc., editor at large for Christianity Today, and the author of Reconciliation Blues: A Black Evangelical's Inside View of White Christianity. *Mark Galli is managing editor of* Christianity Today *and author of* Jesus Mean and Wild: The Unexpected Love of an Untamable God, Francis of Assisi and His World, *and other books. "Harder than Anyone Can Imagine," was first published in* Christianity Today, *April 2005, Page 36.*

■ Open Up

Select one of these activities to launch your discussion time.

Option 1

Discuss these icebreaker questions:

- Describe a cross-cultural experience you've had, whether overseas or among a different cultural group here in our country. What was challenging about it? What did you gain from it?

- Is your own cultural heritage important to you? If so, in what ways is it meaningful in your life? If not, why not?

- How would you describe the racial or cultural status of your area? Reflect together on how it compares or contrasts with the racial makeup of your church.

Option 2

Select one member of your group to lead this activity while the rest of you participate.

First, designate three areas of your meeting space or an outdoor area (such as couches, corners, doorways, or trees) to represent *positive, negative,* and *neutral.* The activity is simple: the leader will say a word and each group member must immediately decide how he or she feels about that word. Participants should then quickly go to the area that represents their feeling, either positive, negative, or neutral. There is to be no talking during the activity (other than the leader); you can discuss your thoughts and opinions after the experience is done.

When everyone is ready, the leader should read aloud the following words, allowing participants to move after each one: *diversity, racism, integration, minority, traditions, multiculturalism, power, ethnicity, heritage, prejudice, culture,* and *segregation.*

After the activity, discuss how you responded similarly or differently to the various words. Talk about these questions:

- Which of these words did you feel especially negative about? Why?
- Depending on one's life experiences, people can view these words and their meanings very differently. Which of the words do you think might mean something very different to someone whose life (race, cultural background, socioeconomic status, and so on) is very different than your own? Explain?

■ The Issue

On "Meet the Press" in 1960, Martin Luther King Jr. was questioned about the lack of white members in his traditionally black church. He answered by saying:

> I think it is one of the tragedies of our nation, one of the shameful tragedies, that eleven o'clock on Sunday morning is one of the most segregated hours, if not the most segregated hours, in Christian America. I definitely think the Christian church should be integrated, and any church that stands against integration and that has a segregated body is standing against the spirit and teaching of Jesus Christ, and it fails to be a true witness. But this is something that the church will have to do itself.

- Do you agree with Dr. King that it is "shameful" that churches are so racially segregated? Why or why not?

Though overt racism may exist in some corners, it is usually not the main reason behind the racial segregation of churches in America today. The vast majority of committed Christians in America attend churches that are racially homogenous for reasons other than racism or overt prejudice.

- What are some of the reasons people often attend churches that are racially and culturally homogeneous? Consider both positive and negative reasons.

(To help you brainstorm, contrast a culturally homogenous church experience with some of the difficulties or discomforts you might experience if you were to regularly attend a church with a dominant cultural identity very different from your own.)

It is obvious to even the casual observer that the church is segregated. All ethnic communities have a tendency to worship in their own language and style. What would you do if someone from another race or nationality walked into your church and sat next to you during Sunday morning worship? Would you make the effort to find out more about them? Or would you expect them to suppress their cultural expression and blend in with the style of your church? It is important that we as a church recognize where we are in this socio-spiritual dilemma and then do what we can to follow the biblical mandate to be the people of God despite our cultural differences. The truth is that it is not as easy as it sounds.

■ Reflect

Take a moment to read Isaiah 56:3–8; Acts 2:42–47, 4:32–33; and Galatians 3:26–28 on your own. Jot down some notes about how these passages relate to issues of race and culture in the church. What are the key ideas in each passage? What questions do these verses raise for you?

SESSION 5: MULTIRACIAL CONGREGATIONS

■ Let's Explore

Racial unity is a deliberate part of God's plan for his church.

Read these statements aloud:

—God's desire for us is that we become the "one people of God."

—We need to ignore the race issue and focus on evangelism and other priorities in the church.

—We may lose our cultural heritage if we move toward racial integration in our churches.

—We should substitute the church culture as the new and acceptable culture in place of our own racial identities.

—Our church identity should be transcultural.

—The church should be marked through servanthood, not race.

—Multiracial unity in our congregations will cause more problems than good.

- Which of the statements above do you strongly agree or strongly disagree with? Which statement best reflects your personal point of view on this issue?

Read Isaiah 56:3–8. The God of the Old Testament is the same as the God of the New Testament. However, in the Old Testament God works primarily with the nation of Israel, his chosen people, and secondarily with the world around them. In the New Testament God does the same with the church. In Isaiah 56:3–8 God proclaimed blessings on all nations. He also comforted two categories of people who were marginalized by the religious majority.

- Which two groups of "outsiders" are mentioned in this passage? What are some "outsider" groups in our society today? How can the church bring those people into the church?

- Imagine someone from one of the outsider groups you mentioned attending your church. Which aspects of your church culture might be difficult for them to relate to or participate in? What might your church need to change to better accommodate outsiders?

- Based on Isaiah 56:3–8, what is God like? What does God value? How often do you think of God in this way? Explain.

No matter what our differences are, we are one in God's house because the blood of Christ unites us.

Some people talk about being "color blind" as a way to overcome racial problems or prejudice. Others take a different tack and use terms like *multiculturalism* and *diversity* to stress cultural distinctives and focus on what makes groups of people unique.

- What are the strengths and weaknesses of these approaches? Is it a good thing to be "blind" to our racial or cultural differences—to act as if they don't exist? On the flip side, is it divisive to emphasize our differences? Explain.

SESSION 5: MULTIRACIAL CONGREGATIONS

Mark 11 records that Jesus was so saddened and angry by the commercialization of the temple that he drove the moneychangers out and quoted from Isaiah 56:7, saying that the house of God was "a house of prayer for people from all nations" and was to be revered accordingly. There was to be no distinction among people when they came into the house of God, so that God could dwell again in purity among his people.

Paul expands upon this idea in a discussion about Jews and Gentiles. Read Galatians 3:26–28.

- Paul is not suggesting that cultural or societal differences no longer exist for Christians, but rather he is emphasizing a higher truth that supersedes our differences and unites God's people. In what ways are we "all the same in Christ Jesus"? What common bonds unite us? Be specific.

- We don't have to ignore our uniqueness to be God's people. Rather, we can enhance our cultural uniqueness by helping the church grow closer to the pattern of Christ. How can we use our differences to contribute to the church rather than to divide it? Share specific examples and ideas.

Racial unity is demonstrated when we lay down our power and share in all things.

Bill Hybels raises the issues of power versus servanthood and power versus justice and inclusion. When power is vested in a limited number of elite people, others are excluded. In the church, power is demonstrated when God's people come together.

Read Acts 2:42–47 and 4:32–33.

The early church demonstrated the spirit of unity after they were touched by the miraculous power of the Holy Spirit. Acts 2:7–11 tells us that these people were from different racial backgrounds and spoke different languages. The coming of the Holy Spirit empowered them and brought them together in a wonderful way. This did not mean their ethnic identities were blurred, but amidst their diversity it gave them, as Hybels says, "more visibility." They were all able to work together with a common and divine purpose. Acts 2 shows us how they shared all things with each other. Acts 4 tells how they demonstrated both great grace and great power when the boundary walls of ethnic divisions came down.

- Hybels talks about the "power of Christian community" that "draws different people together." What do you think the essence of that power is? Describe what you think the church can do to demonstrate this power to the world around us. What part does racial unity play in this?

Rah talks about people "laying down their power to come into God's presence together." As fellow believers in Christ, there is power in unity. But laying down power does not come easily to any of us. Rah points out, "Laying down power will mean different things for different communities." Hybels expressed that language about laying down power "has been a turnoff" because it didn't reflect the way his church viewed leadership roles.

- What's your personal reaction to the idea of "laying down power"? How do you think your church would respond to this idea? Why?

- In what ways might power (leadership, control, influence) need to be surrendered in a church in order for it to be more racially and culturally diverse? How would laying down power aid racial harmony?

■ Going Forward

- If Jesus were to visit your church today, what do you think he would say to your congregation about the issue of racial unity?

In the article, Noel Castellanos comments that "the churches have to accept the challenge." Here are three steps you could take to accept the challenge and begin the process of understanding other people:

1. Attend a church service in your community that includes those of a different ethnic background than your own. Write down your thoughts and impressions. What things made you feel uncomfortable? What things did you find positive?

2. Initiate unity services with that church (once a month or once in six months) so church members begin to show the world that Christ's church is not segregated. Ask members to discuss their reactions in small group situations. Plan further steps to initiate racial integration in our churches.

3. The next time someone from another race comes into your church, take steps to make that person feel welcome. Get others involved too. Demonstrate to others what Jesus might do.

- Which of these ideas appeals to you personally? Or what is another idea you have for how God is leading you to accept this challenge?

CURRENT ISSUES: THE FUTURE OF THE CHURCH

What is our responsibility in a world filled with disasters, terrorism, and tragedy?

SCRIPTURE FOCUS

Matthew 10:5–16, 25:31–46

James 2:14–26

SESSION 6

FIRST RESPONDERS

■

Terrorist attacks. Hurricanes, tsunamis, and cyclones. Suicide bombings. Floods, earthquakes, and tornadoes. School shootings. Droughts and famines. Wars and genocide.

These are just some of the events that have dominated headlines in recent decades. What will be the tragedies of the future? And how will the church respond?

When tragedy strikes, our response is often to rail at God with our *whys*. We may feel angry at injustice we see or we may feel deep compassion for those in need, but how often do we move feeling to *doing*? Yet there are some in the church who immediately spring into action, serving as models for us all. One such example was the response to Hurricane Katrina by much of the Christian community in the American South. In this study, you'll read about the Christian response to the hunger, homelessness, and heartache that ensued after the storm ravaged the Louisiana and Mississippi coast.

When tragedy strikes, Christians have an opportunity to take responsibility and care for those in need. How will we help those in crisis? How sacrificial does God want us to be? And what is our responsibility to help those whose behavior makes it difficult to help? Rather than asking, "Why did this happen?" this study asks, "How can we respond in a way that most glorifies God?"

■ Before You Meet

Read "The Sunday After" from *Christianity Today*.

THE SUNDAY AFTER

What Gulf churches were doing on the first Lord's Day after Katrina.

by Tony Carnes in New Orleans and Pascagoula, with Rob Moll

It is noon, time for the shift change for the police in New Orleans' Sixth District, on the first Sunday since Hurricane Katrina struck. Hy McEnery, a Baptist chaplain with Child Evangelism Fellowship, knows he has to encourage the officers to keep going. In the face of the unrelenting pressure, danger, and temptation caused by the chaos in the Big Easy, some officers have committed suicide. Others have joined the looters. Still more have simply left their posts.

These men, although still on the job, have been "crunched," as one puts it. The ones going off duty on this hot, sunny day look weary and smell of oily water and decayed matter. The ones coming on look just as weary and smell only a little better.

McEnery picks Psalm 69, discussing the topic, "Why have the waters overwhelmed me?" The officers stand quietly as McEnery tells them that God will help them "in the deep mire." Jesus, he says, can give them refreshing waters.

Work and Worship

As many Gulf churches as could tried to provide spiritual encouragement. At Woodland Baptist's service in Hammond, Louisiana, Leon Dunn preached on Jeremiah 29 and God's plans for his people. He said, "My idea of camping out is the Holiday Inn. But this storm didn't catch God by surprise.

SESSION 6: FIRST RESPONDERS

"I don't care how dark the night is, let's keep helping our neighbor and keep Christ first. God has a plan. Not only God has a plan, we still have a purpose. I will be honest with you: it has been a difficult season. But our purpose hasn't changed since last Sunday. God put us here to give a cup of cold water to our brother." Woodland so far has served eighteen thousand meals right out their front door.

Many pastors and church members are still dealing with shock. At the Southern Baptist disaster station in First Baptist Church in Pascagoula, the building is relatively undamaged, although almost every building from it down to the beach was heavily damaged or destroyed.

Associate pastor Dennis Smith stayed at the church during the storm. Early Monday morning, while it was still dark, a twenty-two-foot storm surge hit the city. Smith prayed and watched. The water surged all the way to the church door and then played out. Smith started thinking about the future after the storm. He prayed, "Lord, you gave a home to me the first time, and you'll give it back to me."

Smith went over to his house after the storm. Southern Baptist crews were cleaning it up and hauling out the wreckage. They hauled out his old roll top desk and opened the bottom right drawer to his Bibles. As they showed the pastor the Bibles one by one, Smith broke down. "Most of my stuff had to be thrown it into the trash," Smith tells *Christianity Today*, and points to a book. "That was my first Soul Winner's Bible."

Most of the wreckage had to be discarded to prevent mold from growing in the house.

Smith finds it hard to sleep at night. He worries over a missing church member or the relief effort. "Last night, two church members were very near death from illness."

Other local churches are going full throttle on attending to physical needs. In Metairie, volunteers with Victory Fellowship bring in four trailer loads of supplies. The local deputy sheriff says in amazement, "Guys, you have done more in an hour than FEMA [Federal Emergency Management Agency] has done all this time."

Several Christian groups are out rescuing people from flooded buildings. *Christianity Today* spent time with a ragtag group of Veterans Hospital patients, local residents from New Orleans, and a small contingent from outside churches, such as Quentin Road Bible Baptist Church of Lake Zurich, Illinois. Leading them are McEnery and James Caffin, an experienced rescuer who has come from Dallas.

The rescuers, who have been driving themselves from sunup far into the night, face their task exhausted and with their nerves on edge. But they persevere. "When these people come onto the boat and hug me," Caffin says, "I feel like I am being hugged by Christ."

The rescuers are scrounging for gas, because lives can be counted by the number of gallons on hand. "Each full tank of gas in the boat is twenty to twenty-five lives that are rescued," Caffin calculates.

The Big Picture

The Southern Baptists are a presence to contend with in the South, and that is a good thing this week. With a strong and long-established presence in the region, they have set up disaster stations up and down the Gulf Coast. Their disaster relief effort is a marvel of efficiency, timetables, trucks, mobile ham radio centers, and mass production of meals. Their equipment gleams and their people are fresh and beaming due to a constant rotation of teams of volunteers bringing order to chaos. CT visited Southern Baptist centers in Mobile, Alabama; Biloxi and Pascagoula, Mississippi; and Hammond, Louisiana.

As the third-largest relief organization in North America, the Southern Baptists' North American Mission Board works closely with the Red Cross and the Salvation Army.

By Wednesday, two days after the hurricane, the North American Mission Board had one thousand volunteers preparing meals, operating two Red Cross kitchens and two kitchens for the Salvation Army.

Burton says Southern Baptist churches are the main means through which the Convention will provide relief. Those that are relatively undamaged will provide shelter both for the hurricane refugees, as well as for relief workers.

Tony Carnes is is a senior writer and news reporter for Christianity Today. *He lives in New York City and specializes in political and urban news coverage. "The Sunday After" was first published in* Christianity Today, *October 2005.*

SESSION 6: FIRST RESPONDERS

■ Open Up

Select one of these activities to launch your discussion time.

Option 1

Discuss these icebreaker questions:

- Most Americans, Baby Boomers and older, remember exactly where they were and what they were doing when they learned of President John F. Kennedy's assassination. So what about the more recent tragedies of our time? Do you remember where you were when you heard about the 9/11 terrorist attacks (2001), the Indian Ocean earthquake and tsunami (2004), the 7/7 bombings of the British subway/bus system (2005), Hurricane Katrina (2005), or the Myanmar cyclone (2008)? Which of these tragedies do you remember most distinctly? What images stick in your mind from those events?

- What are some other human-caused tragedies or natural disasters that have taken place during your lifetime and that stand out in your mind (global or local)? Brainstorm together and create a master list as a group.

- Imagine you could predict the future: what tragedies or crises do you think might happen around the world in the next ten or twenty years?

Option 2

Have you ever been the first on the scene when someone's been injured? Have you ever been called on to help someone who's sick or in pain? Evaluate how strong your "first responder" instincts are and gather around a computer with an internet connection to take a quiz together. Select one of these web sites for your quiz:

> www.firstaidweb.com/firstaid_quiz.html: twenty True/False questions on general first aid knowledge

www.packyourgear.com/firstaidquiz.aspx: ten multiple choice questions about first aid that might be needed on a family camping trip

pediatrics.about.com/cs/quizzes/l/bl_firstaid_qz.htm: four to twenty multiple choice questions, from "easy" to "expert," about providing first aid to children

How well did you do on the quiz? Discuss how adequately prepared you think you'd be to serve as a first responder on the scene of a tragedy. Then talk about this question:

- Imagine you could predict the future: what tragedies or crises do you think might happen around the world in the next ten or twenty years?

■ The Issue

- What is your first response when something difficult happens to you? What if something difficult happens to others? Do you respond the same way? Why or why not?

If you've ever lived through a natural disaster or large-scale tragedy, your immediate response probably wasn't to spend most of your time wrestling with philosophical ideas about why God allows tragedy. Instead, you were probably completely focused on trying to figure out where your next meal would come from, where you'd live, and how you'd support your family.

Jesus asked us to put ourselves in the place of those who are suffering when he gave us the Golden Rule and told us to treat others as we'd like them to treat us. Stories such as the Good Samaritan expand our definition of who is our neighbor, demanding that we *do* something rather than rant or lay blame.

Of all the stories coming out of disasters like the Myanmar cyclone, the flooding of the Mississippi river valley, Hurricane Katrina, or 9/11, the ones of love and generosity have touched our hearts the most. We all have a sense that we want to do something to make things better. Our faith calls us to action.

- When you are in crisis, do you most want answers or practical help? Can practical help provide answers? Why or why not?

■ Reflect

Take a moment to read Matthew 10:5–16, 25:31–46; and James 2:14–26 on your own. Write down words or phrases that are particularly challenging to you. Take notes about the key ideas in each passage; record any questions these verses raise about responding to tragedies and helping those in need.

■ Let's Explore

In times of tragedy and in everyday life, our faith is demonstrated by our deeds.

Read these statements:
—My deeds are not as important as my beliefs.
—My beliefs are not as important as my deeds.
—My beliefs and my deeds are inseparable—one validates the other.
—My beliefs are completely separate from my deeds.
—My deeds reveal my beliefs.

- Which do you most agree with? Why? What is at stake in each position?

Read James 2:14–26.

- As you read this passage, did anyone come to mind who exemplifies this type of faith? Describe someone you know whose actions—especially in responding to those in need—speak loudly about his or her faith. What stands out to you about that person?

Many of us are proud of standing for our faith. We are glad to fight for our rights as Christians and proclaim loudly what we believe. But what is going to make others believe what we say is true? According to James, it is our deeds. What we do is going to be more powerful than what we say.

- Do you agree that actions speak louder than words? If so, consider your own response (or lack of response) to local or global needs and tragedies. What message have your actions been sending? What message would you *like* to send?

In an article, World Vision's President Rich Stearns looks toward the future challenges the church will face in the areas of relief and development and asks,

> Will followers of Christ lead? . . . Will the faith community lift the needs of the poorest of the poor higher on their priority list—higher than our building programs, our church-growth seminars, and our music ministries? Will we demonstrate the love of Christ so convincingly in our concern for "the least of these" that we actually begin to change the way Christians are viewed by the secular world?

- How would you respond to Stearns's question? In what specific ways do you hope the church will lead?

SESSION 6: FIRST RESPONDERS

During the aftermath of Hurricane Katrina, *The Advocate* carried an article by William Taylor called, "Churches Rally to Aid Refugees." In this article he quotes Bishop Robert W. Muench of Baton Rouge:

> Books have been written to explain why bad things happen to good people, but Muench said the volunteers he saw provide a more tangible answer to questions of where God is in a tragedy.
>
> "In the midst of this disaster we are seeing a great deal of goodness that people are demonstrating to their neighbor and a great deal of care in that we see the work of God to have a neighborly response to one another," he said.

- What are some specific examples in your local church or in your community of Christians responding to needs with practical actions?

Our actions are to be righteous, even if the people we are helping are not.

Read this illustration together:

You are in your church building for a meeting when a bedraggled man comes in asking for money. He says he doesn't have money for the electric bill; he's so broke that he's worried his family will be kicked out of their apartment. Knowing nothing about the man, you have to make a decision. Should you or your church provide money to a person whom you know nothing about? How can you really know if this man is even trying to provide for his family? What if he wastes the money on alcohol or drugs?

- What do you think you'd do in this scenario? Have you ever been in a situation like this? If so, how did you respond?

Read Matthew 25:31–46.

- How would you summarize this passage in your own words? How would you describe the two groups of people (on Christ's left and right) in practical terms?

Read Matthew 10:5–16

- In Matthew 10:8, Jesus tells his disciples, "I give you these powers freely, so help other people freely." What does that tell us our attitude should be toward those in need? How common is this mind-set among Christians today? Share examples.

Most of us have private standards which guide our thinking about who we help or give money to, such as they must not be on drugs or using alcohol; they cannot be lazy; they should not be criminals; they must at least be *trying* to improve their lives; they must be thankful and appreciative. Some of us may also have standards we don't overtly acknowledge but which do affect our decision making, such as they must not be ugly; they must not smell badly; they must not use gruff or foul language; they must not be Muslim, Buddhist, Hindu, and so on; they must be someone I *feel* compassion for.

- In light of Christ's words about helping "the least" of people and giving "freely," do you think it's okay to have standards guiding who we help? If so, which standards are okay and which aren't?

In an editorial titled "Parable of the Good Church," the editors of *Christianity Today* write,

> He knew that some of the needy would, with just a little help, bounce back quickly. These were always a pleasure to minister to. But some, with deep physical or psychological maladies, would never be able to fully take care of themselves. These were a challenge, but their condition was understandable. And then there were others still, people perfectly capable of bouncing back, of taking care of themselves, but who instead had chosen a lifestyle of dependency and complaint. This last group is nothing but trouble for ministries far and wide. And yet Young realized that all these people needed the compassion of Christ showered on them—even those who, like the nine lepers Jesus healed (Luke 17), would remain forever ungrateful.

Dale Hansen Bourke of Opportunity International says, "So often we judge ministry on efficiency and viability and efficacy . . . [But] Jesus picked the biggest losers. He constantly risked his 'reputation' by helping those who had made poor choices, who were not innocent victims, who were blatant sinners."

- What's your response to the challenge posed by Bourke and by the parable? Who are people in the parable's last group—ungrateful, problematic, difficult, or blatant sinners—that God may be prompting you to help or show compassion toward?

■ Going Forward

In the article "The Sunday After," Leon Dunn said in his sermon on Jeremiah 29, "I don't care how dark the night is, let's keep helping our neighbor and keep Christ first. God has a plan. Not only God has a plan, we still have a purpose. I will be honest with you: it has been a difficult season.

But our purpose hasn't changed since last Sunday. God put us here to give a cup of cold water to our brother."

- Pastor Dunn challenged his congregation to be true to the church's purpose. How would you state that purpose in your own words?

- How would you sum up the church's responsibility to those who are victims of tragedy? How well is your home church fulfilling this responsibility? Share examples of your church's strengths and weaknesses in this area.

- In what specific ways has God challenged you personally through this discussion? What steps would you like to take now—or in response to future tragedies or disasters—to respond to God's calling?

Pray together as a group, asking God to prepare you to respond to needs and tragedies with practical action. Use a newspaper to guide your time of prayer as you talk to God specifically about global and local tragedies, disasters, and crises; invite God to lead you toward specific avenues of response to the issues you pray about.

Notes

CURRENT ISSUES: THE FUTURE OF THE CHURCH

How will the faith of today's younger generations shape the face of the future church?

John 8:31–32, 14:5–7, 17:1–25

EMBRACING ORTHODOXY

■

Watch out, promiscuity! Out of the way, relativism! A wave of young Americans just wants that old-time religion. *Christianity Today* editor Agnieszka Tennant talked with journalist Colleen Carroll about young people devoted to orthodoxy, whom Carroll described in her book *The New Faithful: Why Young Adults Are Embracing Christian Orthodoxy* (Loyola Press, 2002). Throughout the book it is apparent that the concept of—and the person behind—absolute truth has captured the imagination of these "new faithful." Nothing is more countercultural than the assertion of truth in a postmodern society, and this is becoming the rallying cry for faith-filled young Catholics and Protestants who hope to turn the heart of our nation to Jesus Christ.

■ Before You Meet

Read "The Good News about Generations X & Y" from *Christianity Today*.

THE GOOD NEWS ABOUT GENERATIONS X & Y

Watch out, promiscuity! Out of the way, relativism! A wave of young Americans just wants that old-time religion. An interview with the author of *The New Faithful: Why Young Adults Are Embracing Christian Orthodoxy*.

by Agnieszka Tennant

In 2000, a journalist for the St. Louis Post-Dispatch *pitched an idea to the Phillips Foundation Journalism Fellowship Program. Colleen Carroll wanted to examine the attraction of young adults to Christian orthodoxy and their efforts to transform the culture. She won a $50,000 grant, took a year off from the newsroom, and delved into her research, meeting with over five hundred "new faithful," young people devoted to orthodoxy. What she found turned out to be more widespread than she had expected.*

Christianity Today's *Agnieszka Tennant talked with Carroll about her findings published in* The New Faithful: Why Young Adults Are Embracing Christian Orthodoxy *(Loyola Press).*

When did you first become aware of the intense interest that many young people express in Christianity?

I saw signs of it for years. I was noticing things that ran counter to the conventional wisdom about Generation X when I was at Marquette University in Milwaukee. I was there between 1992 and 1996. A lot of what I heard and saw in the media didn't jibe with what I was seeing among my peers. Some of it did, and some of it still does. But I felt that a lot was being left out in the analysis of Generation X and, even later, Generation Y.

What surprised you most in your research?

I was surprised by just how widespread this trend was, how deep it runs in the culture. It wasn't spotty. I had so many stories and sources that I constantly had to turn down people who wanted to tell me their story, which is pretty rare. People were thrilled that someone was noticing something that they were living day after day.

What do you mean by orthodox Christianity?

I use a definition offered by G. K. Chesterton, who said that orthodox Christianity is "the Apostles' Creed, as understood by everybody calling himself Christian until a very short time ago and the general historic conduct of those who heed such a creed." He wrote that in 1908, but it still holds true. One Generation Xer, Andy Crouch, editor of the Christian Vision Project, defined orthodox Christians pretty succinctly as people who can say that creed without crossing their fingers behind their backs.

What about orthodoxy particularly is appealing to Generations X and Y?

You can look at it in two ways. One is sociological. These young adults are reacting in large part against a lot of what they grew up in or what they've seen around them—not only in the media and popular culture but even in their churches. Among Protestants, there is a swing against mainline Protestantism in some cases. Some young evangelicals might be moving into mainline churches looking for liturgy, but they're still committed to the central tenets of evangelicalism and very concerned about being in a church where the Word is preached and not compromised by other concerns.

For Catholics, there is a similar reaction. A lot of Catholics today grew up when the Baltimore Catechism was out and "God is love" was in. They learned a lot about love but they often didn't learn much of anything about the faith. And a lot of them left for a time and came back or rolled along with it until they had a reconversion experience and really looked into the faith. Now they're very committed to unabashedly proclaiming what Catholicism is and rejecting versions of Catholicism they think aren't true to the pope or to the teaching of the church or to Scripture.

In general, there is a reaction against the larger culture—a feeling of being saturated by greed, sex, and all the decadent forces in our culture. But sociology is not the full explanation here. There is a deep spiritual hunger that transcends sociology.

Where does this hunger come from?
The hunger comes from a lot of different places. If you feel like you weren't fed growing up, then you're going to have intense hunger. So some of it is just I didn't get what I needed from my church. Some of it is I didn't get what I needed from my family. Rising divorce rates affected this generation—leading to a breakup of family, breakup of community, a sense of feeling isolated. So all of that has contributed.

Yet, some of this trend, I believe, is just the work of the Holy Spirit, and that's what the young believers will tell you. They'll refuse to chalk it up to sociology or rebellion. The gospel is timeless, and the attraction is timeless.

How does the path of these young believers differ from that of their parents and grandparents?
For one thing, this may be one of the first generations where faith is such a conscious choice. It's not something embedded in their family anymore. I searched far and wide, and I didn't find too many people—even among the ones who had been raised in strict Catholicism or in the evangelical subculture who had never questioned their faith. They just don't have that luxury anymore. The culture questions them every day. I quote Os Guinness saying that on the one hand this situation is great because faith is a conscious choice, and on the other hand that can lead to problems, because if something can be consciously chosen it can be consciously rejected when it becomes inconvenient.

What do the new faithful struggle with in orthodoxy?
The crux of their struggle is how they live the orthodox faith in a culture that is not orthodox. Some struggle with isolation. They want to preserve their beliefs, they want to stay safe, and they want to keep their children safe. But they risk winding up with only friends who think

exactly like they do and taking only jobs where their beliefs will never be confronted. Faith can suffer if your full concentration is on yourself and on just preserving what you've got rather than spreading your talents outward.

The flip side is assimilation, another struggle that the new faithful face. A lot of them are zealous about evangelism, so intent on transforming culture with this gospel that has changed their lives. But they can sometimes become naïve about where and how to do that. They sometimes can see Christian themes and truths in places where they don't exist because they want to see them and want to reach out to the world. That's a great instinct, but there are some media through which the gospel doesn't flow well. There are some song or film genres, for instance, that don't work to spread the Christian message. Sometimes, in their eagerness to spread the gospel, the new faithful can see their own faith get weakened or compromised.

Could you give an example of such zealousness gone awry?
Some young Christian artists incorporate gospel messages into heavy-metal rock songs and horror films. They often have thoughtful reasons for doing so. But in some of these cases, such as a discordant, angry song with Christian lyrics or a grizzly, despairing film with an underlying moral theme, the medium overpowers the message. I think movies and music that show glimpses of the true, the good, and the beautiful, even when they are not overtly evangelistic, are more powerful vehicles for transforming culture.

Which writers or books are these young adults most influenced by?
They seem to be attracted to modern classics. For example, they read C. S. Lewis and G. K. Chesterton. A lot of the Catholics have discovered the earlier writings—those of Thomas Aquinas and Augustine.

How can these committed young believers actually transform our culture without falling into the pitfalls you've mentioned— overzealousness and choosing the wrong media?

They're transforming culture through every career they find themselves in. I focused on those young adults who were in positions of some cultural influence, whether through their jobs or their presence at top universities. That's where I found this trend the strongest. This is counterintuitive, because a lot of secular analysts of religion assume faith is for those who have fallen on hard times and didn't really have a lot of other options. At least in the case of the young adults I wrote about, it's exactly the opposite. They're the best and brightest.

For example?
I can think of one young woman, Mary Naber. She wrote an article on ethical investing for CT ["Christ's Returns," Sept. 3, 2001]. She's a Harvard graduate with a double major in religion and economics. I relate the story in the book how she marched into her pastor's office at an evangelical Presbyterian church in California and told him she wanted to serve the Lord and yet she really was interested in business. She asked him what she was to do with that.

She said, "So I'll probably just go work in a church or be a missionary, right?"

He told her, "No, exactly the opposite. You go into business and you bring the gospel with you." She is aware that she's blessed to have a pastor who would say that.

So she went to Harvard, which is a struggle in itself. There's a strong evangelical community there, but it's Harvard. It's very secular. When she announced to her professors at business school that she wanted to also have a major in religion and somehow combine religion and economics, it didn't go over so well. They pretty much told her it couldn't be done. And like a lot of the young adults I interviewed, that energized her.

She studied ethical investing. She did a regression analysis of the returns of investors who took ethical concerns to heart versus those who invested purely for monetary gain and found that there was no net loss among those who were doing ethical investing. Like Mary, these new faithful relish the opportunity to take all the tools of the secular world and use them for God's glory.

SESSION 7: EMBRACING ORTHODOXY

In the culture that has created *Temptation Island* and *Sex in the City*, did you find that the new faithful buck against sexual immorality and instead find fulfillment in traditional families?

Yes. That was among the most surprising discoveries for me. Sexuality is where ideals meet reality in terms of religious commitment, especially for single young adults. If they want to live their faith, those who are committed to Christian orthodoxy believe they need to save sex for marriage. They believe they need to live in a way that is very different from the way the media portray their peers as living. And that's tough, I think, for single Christians who don't always get a lot of support from the pulpit. Sometimes they may hear the message, but it can be hard to meet other Christians with similar values.

There is an element of rebellion against the culture, and it's strong in the area of sexuality. A lot of them have not always been following this path. A lot have gone with the culture and just found it empty and depressing. In many cases, sexuality got them to turn back to God because things had gone so badly when they followed the world's advice in that area. They started to question everything they were hearing from the popular culture.

Is there one style of worship that these young believers tend to embrace?

Definitely not. They want the hard gospel. They want a preacher or a priest to tell it like it is, to give them morality that they believe is sound and doesn't simply cater to their whims. But when it comes to worship styles, they're more flexible. A lot of them are attracted to contemporary worship that is similar to what you'd see in young adult or Generation X services at larger churches.

Another surprise was how many I found attracted to more traditional or liturgical worship—often the ones who weren't raised with it. I found a surprising number of young evangelicals seeking liturgical worship. Sometimes that led them to a more liturgical church, like an evangelical Episcopal church. Some converted to Catholicism or Eastern Orthodoxy in search of, among other things, liturgical worship. They're attracted to what came before.

One keen observation in the book is that young evangelicals seem to have learned something from Catholics and vice versa. What religious lessons have we swapped?

On the part of Catholics, there's a real attraction to evangelicalism. In the past, and still today, this has resulted in Catholics leaving the Catholic Church to go to evangelical churches where they feel the gospel is being preached with more vigor or clarity.

But in the group that I interviewed, I came across a larger number of young Catholics who saw what they liked about evangelicalism and then brought it into their own parishes. Then you have this fascinating combination of Catholic tradition with an evangelical flair.

For example?

One thing that's becoming more and more popular on Catholic college campuses has been student-initiated Eucharistic adoration, which is obviously about as Catholic as you can get. They adore what they believe is the presence of Christ in the Eucharist—but while doing it, they sing evangelical songs. There is a charismatic flair to the worship, raising of hands. Some sit on the floor; it's casual. You hear evangelical favorites such as "Lord, I Lift Your Name on High."

Another example is a zeal among younger Catholics to spread the gospel. The zeal is also a direct result of Pope John Paul's exhortations to young Catholics to spread the faith. He's a real hero of theirs, and when he stressed evangelism, that's something they really picked up on.

How does the zeal manifest itself? Catholics aren't known for going door to door.

Surprisingly enough, some young Catholics do go door to door! Actually, I've seen a couple of groups that are starting to do that. So when I say that young Catholics are copying evangelicals, they really are. A lot of them are doing things that even, I think, the older generation of Catholics is pretty surprised by, delighted by, and sometimes just confused by.

What are younger evangelicals learning from Catholics?

They sometimes incorporate liturgy into their worship. They look to Catholic social teaching, particularly the teaching of Pope John Paul II, when they're trying to address issues that maybe aren't addressed as much in their churches, issues like cloning or stem-cell research. The emphasis on serving the poor is of real interest to younger evangelicals. I met one young evangelical woman whose husband is a pastor at a Protestant church. When it comes to serving the poor, she just didn't hear enough about that in her church growing up. It wasn't until she started discovering some Catholic social teaching that she began learning about it. Now she works in an ecumenical setting with Catholics and Lutherans and evangelicals. They're all working together to serve the poor, and she has quotes from Mother Teresa on her desk.

Are the new faithful the new ecumenists?

Definitely. In Washington, D.C., there's a vibrant community of young orthodox Christians, many of whom are rising leaders. One evangelical—chief of staff for a congressman on Capitol Hill—told me that Christians can't afford to fight each other there because "our differences seem small compared to the assault of the humanist worldview." And there's the same attitude in Hollywood. I spent some time there and noticed a lot of ecumenism going on between evangelicals and Catholics who are seeking to break into screenwriting or into acting.

How do the new faithful compare to their unbelieving peers?

In many cases, they are the people to whom their peers look to set trends. They are often quite successful. They're sometimes coming from the best schools. A lot of them are in places like Hollywood or on Capitol Hill. So they are not a fringe minority. They are in a minority, but it's a disproportionately influential one.

Also, while they're in the minority, a lot of what they express is what you'll hear from many young adults. I found that the refrains were similar. There is a lot of disdain—for media, marketing, some baby boomer values, even materialism.

For Christians interested in evangelism, that's an important thing to think about. If a lot of these young adults had the same formative experiences and a minority of them were introduced to orthodoxy and fell in love with Christ, then that suggests that there's obviously a hunger that is not found only in this small group.

All in all, isn't orthodoxy an attraction to some in every generation?

You're right. The gospel is always exciting; so is orthodoxy, which is a full expression of the gospel. That's why I hesitate to label the trend simply as something that happened to the children of the hippies who have rebelled by becoming conservative. That's way too simplistic.

Do you have a way of knowing how statistically significant this trend toward orthodoxy is among younger people today?

These things—sexual values, philosophical perspectives, eternal hopes—are difficult to quantify with one overarching number. So I tried to break down the question and address it using a variety of statistics related to the many realms of young adult experience—sexual values, political activism, attitudes on college campuses.

In many of those realms, the statistics indicated that young, orthodox Christians are fighting an uphill battle against the culture and, often, the church. But many statistics also suggest that trends are moving in their favor. In the "Sexuality and Family" chapter, for instance, I cited such studies as the annual UCLA survey of college freshmen, which in 1998 found approval of promiscuity at a twenty-five-year low. Nearly 40 percent of students said they approved of casual sex in 1998, down from a record high approval rate of about 52 percent in 1987. Support for legal abortion also dropped for the sixth straight year in that survey.

I think statistics can give important indications of which way the cultural currents are moving, but I would not attempt to argue that the statistics are uniformly or even predominantly on the side of these young orthodox Christians. But I do argue that they have the potential to make up in influence and zeal what they lack in numbers. I believe their influence on statistical indicators will be reflected in the future.

SESSION 7: EMBRACING ORTHODOXY

> Many statistics suggest that the dissatisfaction these young adults have with secularism and materialism is shared by many of their peers, Christian or not. That suggests that many more in this generation may join this trek toward orthodoxy in years to come.
>
> ---
>
> *Agnieszka Tennant is one of "the new faithful." She was an editor at large for* Christianity Today *and is now pursuing graduate studies at Northwestern University. "The Good News about Generations X & Y" was first published in* Christianity Today, *August 5, 2002.*

■ Open Up

Select one of these activities to launch your discussion time.

Option 1

Discuss these icebreaker questions:

- Which generation do you consider yourself to be a part of: Generation Y (also called Millennials), Generation X, the Baby Boomers, the Silent Generation, or the Greatest Generation?
- What are some of the movies, music, events, or trends that you think shaped your generation?
- What do you see as the main strengths and weaknesses of your generation?

Option 2

Divide your group into three teams; if you are able, try to have a variety of ages represented in each team. Assign each team one of these identities: Generation Y (roughly those born between 1980 and 2000); Generation X (roughly those born between 1960 and 1980); or the Baby Boomers (roughly those born between 1940 to 1960).

Each team should draw a picture of a "typical" person of that generation; along with their picture, teams should list their thoughts on the following generational distinctives:

- What important events shaped this generation?
- What cultural or social trends affected this generation?
- What adjectives (both positive and negative) would you use to describe this generation?
- What movies or music trends shaped this generation?

After about five or ten minutes, gather back together so each team can explain their drawing to the rest of the group. Take some time to add ideas or adjectives to each other's drawings; keep the drawings in the center of your meeting space so you can refer to them during your Bible study.

■ The Issue

In her interview, Carroll attributes much of the swing toward orthodoxy among younger generations of Christians to a reaction against relativism. She says,

> These young adults are reacting in large part against a lot of what they grew up in or what they've seen around them—not only in the media and popular culture but even in their churches.... Some young evangelicals might be moving into mainline churches looking for liturgy, but they're still committed to the central tenets of evangelicalism and very concerned about being in a church where the Word is really preached and where it's not compromised by other concerns.

Carroll goes on to say, "They want the hard gospel. They want a preacher or a priest to tell them like it is, to give them morality that they believe is sound and that doesn't simply cater to their whims."

- Have you witnessed or experienced this reaction to relativism? Share examples you've observed or experienced in your own life.

SESSION 7: EMBRACING ORTHODOXY

- In her interview, Carroll mentions Andy Crouch's definition of orthodox Christians as people who can say the Apostle's Creed "without crossing their fingers behind their backs." What's your response to this definition? What else might you add as other important marks of orthodoxy?

■ Reflect

Take a moment to read John 8:31–32, 14:5–7, and 17:1–26 and jot down some notes about what you observe. What strikes you most about Jesus's words in these passages? What are the key themes and ideas? What questions do these verses raise for you?

■ Let's Explore

Our belief in ultimate truth needs to remain firm in a pluralistic world.

- How have you observed the diminished role of truth in our society? How do you think society's view of truth will affect the church in the next fifty years? Explain.

Read John 14:5–7.

Jesus's statement "I am the way, and the truth, and the life" is the sixth of Jesus's seven "I am" statements in the Gospel of John (6:48, 8:12, 10:9, 11, 11:25, 14:6, 15:1). Bible scholars point out that Jesus is the "way" because he is the "truth" and the "life." Jesus is the embodiment of the Father—who is in his essence truth and life. And through Jesus people can come to God. Most important to this discussion is the stress Jesus puts on the exclusive nature of salvation. All are invited to come, but there is only one way to approach God—through his son, the ultimate truth.

Such exclusivity easily offends our postmodern sensibilities. We live in a time when the greatest crime is to insist that you are right. But this is what Christ does unapologetically. The Bible records seventy-eight times when Christ began a statement with, "I tell you the truth."

- Why is the concept of ultimate truth so offensive in today's society? What are some of the claims, beliefs, or practices of Christianity that others may find offensive?

While it seems especially pervasive in our day, ambivalence, and at times even aversion to truth, is not a new phenomenon. Pilate himself expressed incredulity, not at Jesus's claim to be a king, but at his assertion of truth. John 18:28–40 records Jesus's conversation with Pilate before his execution. In verse 38, Pilate famously asks Jesus, "What is truth?" According to John, it looks like Jesus wasn't given the opportunity to answer Pilate's—possibly sarcastic and possibly earnest—question.

- How do you think Jesus might have answered that question if he were given the chance?

- How should the church answer that question when it's asked by postmoderns today? Explain.

SESSION 7: EMBRACING ORTHODOXY

The emerging church movement among younger Christians today is a response to postmodernism (see session 4). Some have critiqued the emerging church movement for an apparent embrace of postmodern values like relativism; the response of the "young faithful" to postmodernism, on the other hand, is characterized by its strident embrace of absolute truth.

- In what ways do the emerging church movement and the trend of the "young faithful" compare or contrast with each other? Which response to postmodernism have you seen more among young people you know?

Our lives need to stand in marked contrast with the world.
Read John 8:31–32.
Here Jesus ties obedience in one's life directly to knowing the truth. In her research, Carroll found that the new faithful are concerned with how their faith affects both their personal and public lives. To simply assert that there is ultimate truth and that the truth can set you free is not enough. Christians must take the substance of their faith and live it on a day-by-day basis.

- What forms of obedience did Carroll highlight as distinguishing marks of the "new faithful"? What other important life choices and trends among Gen X and Gen Y Christians have you observed?

Carroll says that, in part, this trend toward orthodoxy among younger Christians "is a reaction against the larger culture—a feeling of being saturated by greed, sex, and all the decadent forces in our culture." The conflict with the culture is both a good and bad thing, according to Carroll, who went on to say,

The culture questions them every day. I quote Os Guinness saying that on the one hand this situation is great because faith is a conscious choice, and on the other hand that can lead to problems, because if something can be consciously chosen it can be consciously rejected when it becomes inconvenient . . . The crux of their struggle is how they live the orthodox faith in a culture that is not orthodox. Some struggle with isolation. . . . The flip side is assimilation, another struggle that the new faithful face.

- How has the contrast between orthodox Christian faith and the culture at large been good for the church? How has it been good for your own spiritual maturity?

- Which do you tend to struggle with more in your own reaction to the culture: isolation or assimilation? Explain.

Read John 17:1–26.

In this passage Jesus is praying for his disciples on the eve of his arrest. His desire for their lives is very instructive. God's plan was, not to remove his followers from danger and conflict, but to preserve them in the midst of conflict. In Christ's absence we are to remain as witnesses to truth. It is by this truth that we are sanctified and are truly free.

- In which ways do you see Generation X and Generation Y Christians living out some of the things Jesus prayed for? What pitfalls and challenges might Gen X and Gen Y Christians need to be especially careful of?

- Which aspects of Jesus's prayer stand out to you most as you consider the challenges the church will face in future decades? Why?

SESSION 7: EMBRACING ORTHODOXY

■ Going Forward

Gen Xers are moving into positions of leadership in the church today and in a few decades they'll make up the majority of those in leadership roles in most churches. Members of Generation Y, and even those who are very young children today, will be the leaders of the future church in thirty, forty, or fifty years.

- If you are a member of Gen X or Gen Y, how do you feel God may be calling you to influence and serve his church in the next ten, twenty, or thirty years?

- If you are a Baby Boomer or older, how do you feel God may be challenging you to encourage, support, or mentor Gen X and Gen Y Christians?

- The new faithful are attempting to avoid the pitfalls of both isolationism and assimilation in order to transform culture. They are doing this from within their spheres of influence at work, in society, and in the home. Where are your spheres of influence? What can you do to be a witness to truth?

Pray together, asking God to help you cling to truth and live lives of devoted obedience in a relativistic world.

CURRENT ISSUES: THE FUTURE OF THE CHURCH

Why should we stick it out with a flawed body of believers?

SCRIPTURE FOCUS

Matthew 16:15–18

1 Corinthians 12:12–27

Ephesians 5:21–32

Colossians 3:12–15

Hebrews 10:23–25

SESSION 8

LOVING THE
IMPERFECT CHURCH

■

A significant percentage of those who believe in Jesus Christ do not attend church. Maybe they think the preaching is poor, the people are unfriendly, the music is too old or too new, or they simply would rather stay in bed on Sunday morning than deal with the challenges of church life. Maybe they're turned off by the myriad of problems plaguing the church, like immorality among leaders, cultural irrelevance, disunity, or legalism. Maybe you, too, are wondering if it's worth the effort to be a part of the body.

So why should we bother with the church? Why should we return week after week, committing our hearts and lives to this body of imperfect believers? Why should we join in for the long-haul with a church that's plagued with problems, shortcomings, and obvious flaws?

■ Before You Meet

Read "Why I Return to the Pews" by John Koessler from *Christianity Today*.

WHY I RETURN TO THE PEWS

The church has often left me bemused, bored, or mystified, but I can no more abandon it than I can myself.

by John Koessler

The block that intersected the street where I grew up was called Church Street. On one end was St. Angela's, the Catholic church my friends attended. At the other end was Beulah Baptist, where I first heard the gospel. St. Angela's seemed to be a dark mystery with its statues of Jesus and Mary and its holy smell. Beulah, on the other hand, met in a plain-looking building, with pale walls and blond furniture. It did not smell holy. No statue of Jesus could be found in the place.

One Saturday I walked with my friends to their catechism class. When we arrived at the back door to the church, they told me that I could go no farther because I wasn't a member of the parish. I peered through the glass at the Christ mounted on a pedestal that was attached to the wall. His arms were spread in welcome, but not for me. Instead, he surveyed an empty hall below. His mother hung at the other end. She too had her arms spread, as if inviting an invisible audience to enter their embrace.

I spent several minutes gazing from one to the other, my heart pounding. Surely, at any moment they might climb down and wave me away from the door. I wished I could step into the hall and examine the two figures more closely, but my friends had made it clear: I could not cross the sacred threshold.

When the lesson ended, my friends appeared again in the deserted hallway. They opened the red door and fled the place. The faint scent of holiness escaped with them, clinging like the musty smell on an old woman's wedding dress. I gave the statues one last nervous glance, just to make sure that they had not sprung to life, and went off to play.

Vacation Bible School

Beulah Baptist was at the opposite end of Church Street. I visited there because of a parade that took place during that time of year when summer stretches out like the rest of eternity. I was bored. My friends weren't around, and I couldn't think of anything to do. Suddenly, I heard the sound of music and children's voices. Coming down the sidewalk was a parade made up of wagons, balloons, and someone dressed in a clown suit. A group of children marched behind, waving. One of them ran over to me with a piece of paper inviting me to attend something called vacation Bible school.

This might be a good idea, I thought, though I felt ambivalent about attending. The fact that I didn't attend church didn't make me nervous. The "school" part bothered me. I did not enjoy school. The thought of joining vacation and school into some kind of hybrid seemed perverse, like the pictures one sees in the tabloids of babies reportedly born with the head of a dog and the body of a human. Who wants to go to school on his vacation?

Still, the clown was a hopeful sign. These people seemed to promise that if I attended vacation Bible school I would have fun, an intriguing thought. I had never viewed church as a fun place. Perhaps the Baptist church was more like a circus—all colored lights and sounds and laughter.

Beulah Baptist, however, was all business. On the wall behind the pulpit hung a large metal map of the world, sprinkled with pinpoints of light. I thought this was an odd choice for a decoration, more suited to the United Nations than a church. I learned later that the map served to remind church members of the importance of missions.

The people at Beulah were big on missions. Every day in vacation Bible school, we were treated to a missionary story. I could never remember the names or the locations, but the plot was always the same. Some child realizes that the whole world is going to hell and dedicates himself to becoming a missionary. He leaves his weeping parents behind and goes to a distant jungle land. Communication with the natives is hard because he doesn't know the language. It doesn't help matters that the natives are cannibals. As he tries to tell them about Jesus, whose own story seemed to me to be almost as depressing, the natives capture him, cook him in a pot, and eat him. He is quickly replaced by another missionary who has been inspired by his sacrifice. The moral of the story, as far as I could tell, was: "Come to Jesus and this can happen to you too!"

I did not want to go to a distant country and tell cannibals about Jesus. I didn't even like being more than a block or two from my house. I certainly did not want to be boiled in a pot and eaten.

Beulah also had a weekly children's club, a combination of the Cub Scouts and vacation Bible school. The gospel message, like the church itself, was presented each week in an unadorned, matter-of-fact way. Every Wednesday night we sat on metal folding chairs and listened as one of the leaders described the torments of hell and the beauty of the Cross. The message weighed heavily upon my soul. I knew I was a sinner and destined for hell. My Catholic friends had told me as much. Now, the Baptists were telling me the same.

My own conscience confirmed their accusation. Hadn't I once looked at a picture of Sophia Loren in a negligee? On another occasion, while whirling a jump rope over my head like a helicopter rotor, I struck a sparrow sitting on a fence and watched in horror as its small head sailed across the yard. The headless torso just stood there, frozen in place, and then its little body tumbled to the ground. For these and many other crimes, I knew I deserved to go to hell.

By the end of the lesson, I was sure everyone around me could hear my heart pounding. I knew what was coming. The leader would ask us to "accept Jesus." He told us to lift our hands, "right where we were," and let him know. I was too embarrassed to do it and too afraid not to. What if I was the only sinner in the group? But what if I didn't do it? The speaker had said that this might be my last opportunity. I might walk out the door, die on the spot, and be ushered into a Christless eternity that very night.

In the end, my fear of hell won out over my fear of embarrassment. The metal folding chair groaned slightly as I lifted my hand. The leader asked us to repeat a prayer after him. It was as simple as that. Very neat and businesslike. A few days later, I received a nice letter from the pastor of the church, a man I had never seen, congratulating me on the decision I had made.

I tried to be regular, but I didn't fit in. Most of the kids who attended came for game time. But the only game anybody really wanted to play was dodge ball, and I was terrible at it. Overweight and slow on my feet, I was afraid of the ball. It was more like a half hour of target practice than a game, and it didn't take long for the predators in the group to spot the weak animal in the herd. Eventually, I grew tired of their bullying and stopped attending.

Fast-Food Revelation

Even though I heard the gospel at Beulah Baptist, I encountered Christ—really encountered him—in the back room of a Jack in the Box restaurant. The fast-food joint was a mile from my home, on a block that intersected Church Street coming from the other direction.

I had just graduated from high school and was working the night shift, waiting on customers and cleaning the fryers. I was contemplative by nature, and the midnight shift only intensified my introspective tendencies. The situation in my family was an added burden. My mother was sick, wasting away from an illness that would eventually take her life. My father's long-standing alcoholism was worsening. It did not help matters that my favorite radio station only played the blues after midnight. Before long I felt myself sliding into depression.

At some point my thoughts turned to spiritual matters. I purchased a pack of tarot cards and tried to interpret my future from their obscure symbols. I chanted "Hare Krishna" while scraping the grill, hoping it would give me inner peace. Instead it made me dizzy. I carried on a running conversation with God, muttering to him as I swept. Finally, it occurred to me that the Bible was a spiritual book. My mother had given me one several years earlier while I was attending Beulah Baptist. One evening I dusted it off and brought it to work with me. During my breaks I went into the back room and read the Gospels.

The Jesus I discovered there didn't seem anything like the one I had encountered during my pilgrimage up and down Church Street. This

Christ was not perched above the crowd gazing dispassionately at those below. Nor was he like the drab Messiah I had heard about at Beulah. It did not seem to be drudgery to follow him. Indeed, from what I had read, he had promised that it would not be.

"Come to me, all you who are weary and burdened," he said, "and I will give you rest. Take my yoke upon you and learn from me, for I am gentle and humble in heart, and you will find rest for your souls. For my yoke is easy and my burden is light" (Matt. 11:28-30). I sighed with relief as I read these words. Barely twenty, I felt like an old soul too weary of the world to go on.

One night as I was cleaning the restaurant and carrying on a silent conversation with God, I complained, "God, if you're up there, I just want you to know that I wish I had never been born!" I didn't really expect him to reply.

As soon as the thought formed in my mind, I noticed someone waiting at the drive-through window. As I came closer, I recognized him as a local "Jesus freak" named Dave. He said very little as I waited on him. When I gave him his change he grinned and handed me a piece of paper.

"If being born hasn't given you much satisfaction," it said, "try being born again."

Soon I started attending church again. This time it was at Glad Tidings, the church Dave attended. Glad Tidings met in a plain brick building that looked a lot like Beulah, only smaller. It had the same blond wood and bare walls, except for the baptistery, which had a picture of the river Jordan in the background. The church's pastor had once been a crane operator, but his real love was studying history. He was a round-faced man who often clapped his hands and stomped his right foot in a sort of "Holy Ghost dance" when he preached. He appeared to be keeping time to angelic music that the rest of us could not hear. Every so often he would cry "glory" with a drawn-out, rumbling conviction that made us think he had seen something that we could not.

He reminisced about the old days, when the Spirit fell and God's people "got the victory." He began every prayer by saying, "Lord, we're a needy people," intoning the words with such gravity, that in that moment we could feel the crushing weight of the congregation's troubles bear down upon us. It took our breath away. We reeled under the weight of it and clutched the pew. We had no idea! We *were* a needy people. God help us!

I had never witnessed anything like it. He frightened and intrigued me at the same time. He whispered. He shouted. He laughed. He wept. During his message, he displayed the entire range of human emotions. When he finished, we came to the altar and wept copiously, repenting of the same sins we had wept over the previous week.

Coming Home

I have attended many churches since then, both as a member and as a pastor. Down through the years I have made a surprising discovery. Most of the Christians I know are disappointed with their churches, finding them either too traditional or too modern. Their sermons are too theological or not theological enough. The people are cliquish. In the end, the root problem is always the same. It's the people.

Yet Sunday after Sunday these believers return to their pews, expecting God to meet them there once again. Some might view such attendance as an act of futility or an exercise in wishful thinking. I believe it is a work of grace.

The author of *The Message* and veteran pastor Eugene Peterson has written that when we get serious about the Christian life, we usually find ourselves in a place and among people that we find incompatible. "That place and people," Peterson explains, "is often called a church. It's hard to get over the disappointment that God, having made an exception in my case, doesn't call nice people to repentance."

A few years ago I returned to the neighborhood where I grew up. I drove by St. Angela's and saw the door through which my friends had entered so many times to participate in the sacred mysteries of their faith. It looked like it needed a new coat of paint. I wanted to see if the statues of Jesus and Mary were still in their old place, dispassionately beckoning to the multitudes to enter their cold embrace. I felt the old fear and did not get out of my car. I wondered if the smell of holiness still clung to the place.

When I drove by Beulah Baptist, I decided to stop in. I thought they might like to know how one of their Wednesday night clubbers turned out. It had taken a long time, but the prodigal had finally come home.

The pastor welcomed me with professional friendliness and listened politely as I told my story. He looked tired and distracted, perhaps by the work he could have been doing if his time were not being taken up by this unexpected visitor. When our visit was finished, he thanked me for coming and retired to his study. I found my own way out.

It has been nearly four decades since I first went looking for Christ on Church Street. The place where I worship today is neither mysterious nor drab. Its message, still rooted in the hope of the Cross, is consistently positive. Its décor is corporate, its music unrelentingly chipper. I like it.

There are times, though, when I am filled with a quiet longing for the shadow of mystery and the unsettling scent of holiness. In many ways, I am still waiting for the Spirit to fall and for God's people to "get the victory." Wednesday night's children have all grown and gone and the dodge balls have long since been put away. After all these years, there are still times when I feel like an unwelcome visitor. Nevertheless, I decided long ago to cast my lot with the church. It has probably failed me as many times as I have failed it, but I will not abandon it. I could not, without abandoning myself.

John Koessler serves as chair and professor of pastoral studies at Moody Bible Institute. He is the author of several books, including his memoir A Stranger in the House of God: From Doubt to Faith and Everywhere in Between *(Zondervan).* "Why I Return to the Pews" *was first published in* Christianity Today, *December 2004, Page 52.*

■ Open Up

Select one of these activities to launch your discussion time.

Option 1

Discuss these icebreaker questions:

- If you grew up in a church, what was it like? Are your memories of it warm and kind or challenging and harsh? Why?

- If you didn't grow up in a church, what was your opinion about the churches in your area? What stereotypes or ideas, positive or negative, did you have about church and churchgoers? Why?

- What do you love and appreciate most about the local church you're a part of now? Why?

Option 2

You'll need at least twenty wooden blocks, tape, magazines, and permanent markers for this activity.

Form two equal teams and divide up the supplies. One team will be the "Optimists" and the other will be the "Pessimists." Within your team, work together to build a symbolic "church" with your blocks. Decorate the outside of your church with words and images (written, drawn, or from magazines) that describe what the church is like. The Optimists should emphasize all the positive aspects of the church—ways the church is successfully living out the gospel in our world. The Pessimists should zero in on the negative aspects of the church—problems, failings, and flaws that hurt its impact on society and discourage its members.

Take about five to ten minutes to create your churches, then gather back together and have each team explain what you've created and why.

Talk about these questions:

- What stands out to you most from the other team's symbolic church? Why?

- How do you typically think about the church? Do you tend to focus on the positive or dwell on the negative? Why?

■ The Issue

"The church has often left me bemused, bored, or mystified," writes John Koessler. Despite being an author of several Christian books and serving as a leader in a notable evangelical college, Koessler says, "there are still times when I feel like an unwelcome visitor" at church.

- When have you struggled with dissatisfaction, frustration, boredom, or a feeling of not belonging at church? How did you handle those feelings?

Koessler concludes his article with these words: "Nevertheless, I decided long ago to cast my lot with the church. It has probably failed me as many times as I have failed it, but I will not abandon it. I could not, without abandoning myself."

- What reasons have motivated you to stick it out with the church despite frustrations or negative experiences? Explain.

■ Reflect

Take a moment to read Matthew 16:15–18; Ephesians 5:21–32; Colossians 3:12–15; and Hebrews 10:23–25 on your own. Jot down some notes on the key phrases, issues, or ideas you see in these passages. What seems to be most important? What questions do these passages raise for you?

■ Let's Explore

The church is God's creation.
Read Matthew 16:15–18.

Though theologians may endlessly debate over what Jesus meant here in regard to Peter, the controversy which divides Protestants and Catholics often sidetracks us from seeing a simple but profoundly important truth in this verse: *Jesus* builds the church; the church is *his*.

SESSION 8: LOVING THE IMPERFECT CHURCH

- How can we see God's hand at work in the building of his church throughout history? Share examples.

- How have you seen God at work "building" your local church?

Read Ephesians 5:21–32, focusing not on what the passages says about marriage but on what it reveals about Christ and his relationship with his church.

- How does God feel about his church? How does God's regard toward the church compare or contrast with the way you typically regard your local church or the church at large? Explain.

The church is imperfect.

- Although the church is created by God, it is populated with imperfect human beings. When you think about the church in North America, what are some of the obvious "imperfections" in it that bother you? What are some news headlines, scandals, or failings of the church that stand out to you? Why?

- Reflect on the problems in the church and challenges facing the church pointed out by Koessler and in the appendix articles. Which of those issues do you most resonate with? Why?

The church in Corinth had its share of major problems, including disunity, sexual perversion, and lawsuits within the congregation. (You can read more about some of these problems in 1 Corinthians: 1:10–13; 5:1–5; 6:1–8.) Yet it is to this conflict-plagued church that Paul wrote one of the most important passages about how we are to understand our part in God's plan called the church. Read 1 Corinthians 12:12–27.

- What stands out to you most from this passage when you read it in light of the specific problems this church was facing? Do you think Paul is being idealistic or realistic in his description of the church here? Explain.

- Think again of some specific things that bother you about your local church or the church at large; how does this passage speak to the way you should approach those issues? What part may God have for you to play in addressing those failings or shortcomings?

God desires that we be committed to his church.
Read Hebrews 10:23–25 and Colossians 3:12–15.

- How would you describe the level of commitment portrayed in these passages? How does it compare with the way most people today view church participation? Explain.

Being committed to the church is not merely being part of an organization; in real life, this involves being committed to your relationships with specific people—even people who may drive you crazy, hurt you, or frustrate you.

- Do you feel comfortable with this level of commitment described in these passages? Which aspects of Colossians 3:12–15 do you find the most challenging when it comes to your own commitment level to the church? Explain.

When Paul Minear surveyed the New Testament to review its primary descriptions of the church (*Images of the Church in the New Testament*, Westminster John Knox, 1970), he came up with many: community, mission, bride, etc. These many snapshots, he said, could be organized into four major images:

Fellowship of the Forgiven—a camaraderie of fellow travelers who are bound together because all know they are imperfect and all have received forgiveness from God.

People of God—the assembly of those who are God's nation. They take orders from the true commander in chief, they sing national anthems of heaven, they wear the colors of the kingdom, and they live as those on a mission.

Body of Christ—a community that has begun to explore love in deeper dimensions, recognizing their need for one another, their common identity because of Jesus, and their shared mandate to care for one another.

New Creation—those who are living in the power and excitement of being on this side of Easter and knowing that God has begun to transform everything back into its full creational glory. These are the folks who work to transform their neighborhoods to reflect what God wants in human society and who pray fervently for the return of Jesus to make all things new.

- Koessler seems to find these elements of power peeking through the flaws of the churches he has encountered. How might being the "Fellowship of the Forgiven" account for the flaws of the church? What is there about forgiveness, both giving and getting, that sets us apart from the rest of society?

- Which of Minear's descriptions best reflects the way you most often think about the church? How do these descriptions challenge or inspire you in your commitment to the church? Explain.

■ Going Forward

Form pairs to discuss these final questions:

- Why do *you* "return to the pews"?

SESSION 8: LOVING THE IMPERFECT CHURCH

- When you consider the many challenges and opportunities facing the church in the years to come, how do you feel God may be calling *you* to address those issues?

Pray together with your partner by focusing on the challenges facing your local church; focus both on current problems as well as issues you foresee in the years to come. Ask God to give you a steadfast and devoted commitment to his church and guidance as you seek to do your part as a member of the body.